Major
Black
Religious
Leaders
Since 1940

Major Black Religious Leaders

Since 1940

HENRY J. YOUNG

Abingdon
Nashville

MAJOR BLACK RELIGIOUS LEADERS SINCE 1940

Copyright © 1979 by Abingdon

Second Printing 1981

Library of Congress Cataloging in Publication Data

YOUNG, HENRY J 1943–
  Major Black religious leaders since 1940.
  Continues the author's Major Black religious leaders, 1755–1940.
  Includes bibliographical references.
  1. Afro-American theologians. 2. Afro-American clergy.
3. Black Muslims. I. Title.
BR563.N4Y67   230'.092'2   79-11646

ISBN 0-687-22914-6

MANUFACTURED BY THE PARTHENON PRESS AT
NASHVILLE, TENNESSEE, UNITED STATES OF AMERICA

**Dedicated to
the past, present, and future
leadership of the black church**

Contents

Introduction

Major Black Religious Leaders: 1755–1940 examined the
theological views of selected black religionists, seeking to
demonstrate the historic centrality of freedom and liberation in black religious thought. It attempted to show that,
"as opposed to being fixated exclusively with spirituality
and heaven, the black church has been the vanguard of
social, economic, and political activism within the black
community."[1] Beginning with Nathaniel Paul, that volume
systematically evaluated the religious thought of Richard
Allen, David Walker, Nat Turner, Daniel Alexander Payne,
James W. C. Pennington, Henry Highland Garnet, Samuel
Ringgold Ward, Alexander Crummell, Edward Wilmot
Blyden, Henry McNeal Turner, and Marcus Garvey.

The death of Marcus Garvey in 1940 marked a critical
period in the history of black America. Despite the
controversy and disagreement of many blacks, Garvey left a
lasting impression on the black community and on the
nation at large. His effort to relate basic philosophical and
theological ideas to self-respect, self-determination, and
social, economic, political, and community development
has had a sustaining impact on black religious thought.
Garvey was one of the forerunners of the Black Muslim

movement, Black Christian Nationalism, and several other protest ideologies operative in the twentieth century. The present volume begins with the religious philosophy of W. E. B. DuBois, a pivotal figure in many areas of black protest thought during that time. The religious philosophy of DuBois has been much too neglected by scholars and researchers who have examined his social, political, and literary thinking and contributions to the study of history, but have failed to take seriously the religious dimensions of his thought.

The religious leaders discussed in this volume come from diverse professional and denominational backgrounds. They are theologians, religious philosophers, professors, Black Muslim ministers, politicians, and college and seminary presidents. With the exception of DuBois, all the thinkers discussed are clergymen. But DuBois shares with each his appreciation for the contributions of the black church and black religion in the development of blacks in America.

Part I concerns itself with the shift in religious, social, political, educational, and economic thought in the black community, from the period of accommodation and gradualism to that of protest and social activism, discussing the theological and philosophical thought of W. E. B. DuBois, Mordecai Wyatt Johnson, Benjamin Elijah Mays, Howard Thurman, and Adam Clayton Powell, Jr. The thread of freedom and liberation, undergirded with basic philosophical and theological presuppositions, runs through the philosophy of each thinker.

Part II examines the religious and philosophical ideas of the Black Muslim movement in America. It looks at the points of agreement and disagreement between Black Muslims and Black Christian Nationalists as reflected in the thought of Elijah Muhammad, Malcolm X, and Albert B. Cleage, Jr.

Part III investigates black religion, the black church, and protest ideologies. It begins with the death of the Negro church and the birth of the black church, as interpreted by C. Eric Lincoln. It then focuses on Charles Shelby Rooks and his pioneering efforts in theological education. Lincoln's study, The Black Church Since Frazier, is the point of departure for this section. It reveals some of the growing pains the black church experienced in the 1960s while reclaiming its historic legacy by taking the lead in protest and social activism in the black community. Lincoln makes a distinction between the Negro church, as interpreted by E. Franklin Frazier, and the emerging black church.

It required the genius of Martin Luther King, Jr. to bring the Negro church and the black church together into a creative synthesis. In the midst of its growth, King helped the black community hold on to the great legacy, eternal truths, and sustaining Christian principles that are the foundation of both the Negro church and the black church; King challenged racism, segregation, second-class citizenship, unemployment, poverty, and man's inhumanity to man. Part IV interprets the thought of Martin Luther King, Jr. and Jesse Louis Jackson.

Part V assesses the ideas of the leading exponents of black theology in America today, James H. Cone and J. Deotis Roberts, Sr., both of whom are technical theologians.

Using the representative thinkers discussed in this volume, the author's purpose is to show how contemporary black religious leaders and the black church have played a major role in the quest for the complete freedom and liberation of blacks in America. Although each religious leader has a unique and distinct conceptualization of black religion and the black church, the element of protest and the interrelatedness of black religion to the political, social, educational, economic, and cultural structures of society is very apparent.

This volume is written as a sequel to Major Black Religious Leaders: 1755–1940. Neither volume purports to be exhaustive. It was not possible to include every thinker who deserves attention.

PART I

From the Philosophy of
Accommodation and Gradualism
to a Theology of Protest and
Social Activism

Chapter I
W. E. B. DuBois (1868–1963)
*Sociologist, Historian,
Religious Philosopher*

W. E. B. DuBois rose to national prominence in 1903 with the publication of his epoch-making volume *The Souls of Black Folk*.[1] In it he attacked the most distinguished black man in America at that time, Booker T. Washington. He opposed Washington's philosophy of accommodation and gradualism as one of adjustment and submission. He argued that Washington's program accepted the inferiority of black Americans and called on blacks to surrender political power, civil rights, and higher education of youth, and to concentrate their energies on industrial education, the conciliation of the South, and the acculturation of wealth. Washington's program, DuBois felt, significantly led toward disfranchisement and legalization of an inferior status for blacks, and the constant withdrawal of funds from black institutions of higher learning. DuBois argued bitterly that by supporting disfranchisement, Washington, while trying to produce black artisans, businessmen, and property owners, was at the same time denying them the ability to live and defend their rights. Washington insisted that blacks should have self-respect, and yet he counseled them toward civic inferiority. He advocated common school and industrial education and depreciated black institutions of higher learning; Dubois reminded Washington that neither the

17

common schools nor Tuskegee itself could exist without teachers trained in black colleges. He categorized Washington's program as a triple paradox.

DuBois' critique represented a beginning decline in the philosophy of accommodation and gradualism and the emergence of the philosophy of protest. Continuing his opposition to Washington, DuBois organized the Niagara movement in 1905. That group of radical intellectuals denounced Washington's philosophy as a failure.

Early Life and Development

On February 23, 1868, in Great Barrington, Massachusetts, Mary Burghardt DuBois gave birth to a son who was soon to become a maker of history. W. E. B. DuBois was a person of extraordinary intellectual stature—not only an unusual scholar, organizer, and theoretician, but an activist and an exponent of human rights, as well. His cultural impact extended into politics, sociology, history, economics, African studies, literature, race relations, and religion.

He was possessed by an obsession to achieve his maximum intellectual potential. Upon graduation from high school in 1884, DuBois wanted to attend Harvard University, but inadequate funds forced him to do his undergraduate study at Fisk University in Nashville, Tennessee. He taught in the county schools of Tennessee during the summer months, and had firsthand exposure to hardcore racism, black oppression, suffering, poverty, and illiteracy.

After receiving a degree from Fisk in 1888, he entered Harvard as a junior, graduating cum laude in a class of three hundred, with a B.A. in philosophy. One of six commencement speakers, he attracted favorable national attention with his address, "Jefferson Davis: Representative of Civilization." Bishop Potter of New York responded in the *Boston Herald* by saying, "When at the last Commencement of Harvard University, I saw a young colored man appear . . . and heard his brilliant and eloquent address, I said to myself: Here is what an historic race can do if they have a clear field, a high purpose, and a resolute will."[2]

DuBois had a special fondness for philosophic speculation and had hoped to pursue it at the graduate level. His studies with Josiah Royce and George Santayana stimulated his thirst for philosophy, but William James, with his pragmatism, and Albert Bushnell Hart, with his research methods, turned DuBois from philosophic speculation to the social sciences, and he applied these to his lifelong study of the black American.

DuBois was a pioneer in sociological studies. Sociology had not been developed sufficiently to gain recognition at Harvard at the time he was writing his dissertation, "The Suppression of the African Slave Trade to the United States of America, 1638–1870." That dissertation, written and researched under the direction of Albert Bushnell Hart, was published in 1896 as the first volume in the Harvard Historical Studies series.

Having studied under some of the leading scholars at Harvard, DuBois sought to broaden his education by entering a European university. After a considerable effort to secure funds, he was awarded a Slater Fund Fellowship to pursue graduate studies abroad. From 1892 to 1894, he traveled extensively in Europe and studied history and economics at the University of Berlin. When he returned to the United States, he joined the faculty of Wilberforce University in Ohio as professor of the classics. He received the Ph.D. degree from Harvard in 1896. The next year he taught sociology at the University of Pennsylvania and he was then invited to join the faculty at Atlanta University.

Religious Philosophy

It was during DuBois' tenure as professor of sociology at Atlanta that he developed his most profound religious

19

insight into God's justice and the suffering of black Americans. Based on his educational background, DuBois approached religious questions from a philosophical, sociological, historical, psychological, and functional perspective. This approach is evident in his famous poem, "A Litany of Atlanta," written in 1906 while he was traveling by train from Alabama to Atlanta.

DuBois had been in Lownes County, Alabama, completing a study on a black-belt community, authorized by the United States Commission on Labor, when he received news of the Atlanta riot and immediately had set out for Atlanta.[3]

The riot started on September 22, 1906, and was one of the most outrageous instances of organized violence of that decade against black Americans. The press had been launching a local political campaign against blacks in Atlanta, with black disfranchisement as an issue. When on September 24, the blacks resorted to effective self-defense, police actively joined the riots. Ten blacks and two whites were killed and sixty blacks and ten whites were seriously injured. The militant black publication, *Voice of the Negro*, was forced to close, and its editor, J. Max Barber, fled to Chicago for his life.[4] "A Litany of Atlanta" is a theological and philosophical appraisal of the riot and of the tension between God's justice and the problem of black suffering. It depicts the centrality of DuBois' religious philosophy.

God and Justice

In this epic poem, DuBois began with a plea to God for help and support for black Americans facing death, oppression, despair, and suffering, both in Atlanta and in the nation at large. He acknowledged the weakness and lack of power in the black community. When it encountered injustices from the white community, and the police had joined the mobs during the riot, the blacks had nowhere to turn but to God. DuBois then said, "We are but

weak and human men. When our devils do deviltry, curse
Thou the doer and the deed: curse them as we curse them,
do to them all and more than ever they have done to
innocence and weakness, to womanhood and home."[5]
Here DuBois meant that someone has to pay a penalty for
the deaths, afflictions, oppression, and despair of blacks.
He asked God for vengeance, but he reflected further on this
problem and asked the questions: Who is more guilty? Who
made white oppressors? Who nursed them in crimes
against blacks and fed them on injustice? As he considered
the sovereignty and omnipotence of God and his complete
control over the world, DuBois came to challenge the
justice of God.

He asked, "Is this Thy justice, O Father, that guilt be
easier than innocence, and the innocent be crucified for the
guilt of the untouched guilty?" Continuing his challenge,
he asked, "Wherefore do we pray? Is not the God of the
fathers dead? . . . *Awake, Thou that sleepest!*" These
pessimistic questions and this reasoning about God are
based on empirical reality and philosophic metaphysical
conceptualization; for DuBois, the reality of the suffering of
blacks challenged the basic presuppositions about God. If
God were a god of love, righteousness, mercy, omnipotence, and impartiality, then why did he permit the Atlanta
riot and other crimes against blacks? DuBois asked, "Doth
not this justice of hell stink in Thy nostrils, O God? How
long shall the mounting flood of innocent blood roar in
Thine ears and pound in our hearts for vengeance?"[6]

DuBois, in his dialogue with God, described black
Americans as bewildered and passion-tossed—mad with
the madness of a mobbed, mocked, and murdered people.
And straining before the throne of God, DuBois captured
the ethos of black Americans, "We raise our shackled
hands and charge Thee, God, by the bones of our stolen
fathers, by the tears of our dead mothers, by the very blood
of Thy crucified Christ: *What meaneth this?* Tell us the
Plan; give us the Sign!"[7]

21

DuBois could not perceive God's possible purpose in permitting blacks to suffer injustice. He wanted God to manifest himself and to demonstrate his justice, love, mercy, and sovereignty, in support of the black community. He challenged God to be no longer blind and deaf to the suffering of blacks. "Surely Thou too art not white, O Lord, a pale, bloodless, heartless thing?" If God wouldn't help black Americans, what were they to do? To whom were they to turn? DuBois demanded that God speak and show them the way out of suffering and oppression. He said that God could no longer afford to be silent, because "Thy silence is white terror to our hearts!" In asking God for direction, DuBois recognized that the black community really had no place to go. He realized that the North represented greed, exploitation, and racism, and that the South represented blood, slavery, and oppression. He asked, Are we to go to death or life? To death, he said, "Amen! *Welcome dark sleep!*" And to life, he said, "But not this life, dear God, not this. Let the cup pass from us, tempt us not beyond our strength."[8]

What did DuBois' continued challenge and interrogation of God mean? It shows that he pushed to the heart of the religious quest, *fides quaerens intellectum,* which is translated to mean "faith seeking understanding." He insisted upon making existing presuppositions about God more intelligible in the face of the empirical reality of the conditions that stood in direct contradiction to God's nature. DuBois demanded an answer from God; but did he get his answer? He realized that his questions were normal, human, and quite appropriate but could not fully be resolved. He did not succumb to defeatism, agnosticism, atheism, cynicism, or nihilism; rather he discovered a deeper level of God-consciousness, resulting in a new commitment and dedication to God. He concluded, "Thou art still the God of our black fathers, and in Thy soul's soul sit some soft darkenings of the evening, some shadowings of the velvet night. . . . *Vengeance is mine; I will repay,*

22

saith the Lord!"[9] Since vengeance belongs to God, did DuBois wait for God to correct the imbalance between God's justice and the suffering of black Americans? The answer to this and other pertinent questions concerning DuBois' religious philosophy can be found in his understanding of black religion.

Black Religion and the Black Church

DuBois' essay "Of the Sorrow Songs," in his classic *Souls of Black Folk* touches the depth of black religion and reveals how black Americans have maintained integrity with God and themselves and have made an undying effort toward achieving freedom and liberation, in spite of the contradiction between God's justice and their suffering. "Through all the sorrow of the Sorrow Songs there breathes a hope—a faith in the ultimate justice of things." Underneath his challenges and interrogations of God in "A Litany of Atlanta," resided DuBois' belief in an ultimate justice—an affirmation of faith that transcends empirical situations. At some point in the eschatological future, God's righteousness, justice, love, and mercy will prevail. As he identified with the tradition of the makers of black religion in the flight toward that future, DuBois realized that his feelings, along with those of others, had been a mixture of despair, triumph, calm confidence, faith in life, faith in death, and the assurance of boundless justice. And that, ultimately, the hope of black religion is that, sometime and somewhere, black Americans will be judged by their characters and not by the color of their skin.[10]

In attempting to accomplish this task, the efforts of black Americans have been to maintain identification and sensitivity to their ethnicity and heritage, as well as to function within the larger society. The black man in America simply wishes to make it possible for a man to be both black and an American, without being crushed and spit upon by his fellows and without having the doors of opportunity closed roughly in his face.[11]

23

DuBois perceived the black church as the center of the black community and the most viable agent for full emancipation. He thought of it as a religious institution with social, economic, educational, and political implications.

The black church originated in the African forest and was transplanted into American soil. Contrary to the position of E. Franklin Frazier that "it is impossible to establish any continuity between African religious practices and the Negro church in the United States,"[12] DuBois contended that the black church functions as the avenue of continuity with Africanism. It also has served as the source of social activism within the black community, from its inception in America as an "invisible institution," until its existence today as an organized institutional structure. DuBois appreciated this aspect of the black church and viewed it as the force toward the realization of change within the black community.

Contribution

W. E. B. DuBois was an unusually productive person. Many of his writings and publications still remain as landmarks in race relations and Afro-American studies. After the completion of his doctoral dissertation, hailed as the first scientific historical study produced by a black American, DuBois soon became an authority on Afro-Americanism. Continuing this interest in sociology, he wrote *The Philadelphia Negro: A Social Study*, published by the University of Pennsylvania Press.

Many of his insights included in *The Souls of Black Folk* are unsurpassed. It was by far one of the most important books published in the twentieth century. James Weldon Johnson indicated that it would have "a greater effect upon and within the Negro race in America than any other single book published in the country since *Uncle Tom's Cabin*."[13]

W. E. B. DUBOIS (1868–1963)

DuBois wrote more than twenty-one books, more than one hundred pamphlets, essays, and articles, and edited over fifteen volumes. These writings expand into various disciplines and areas of life: politics, economics, race relations, literature, religion, sociology, history, African studies, Afro-American studies, and education. For many years he wrote weekly columns for the *Pittsburgh Courier*, the *Chicago Defender*, the *San Francisco Chronicle* and the New York *Amsterdam News*. He was organizer and editor of the *Atlanta University Publications*, founder and editor of *The Crisis*, member of the editorial board of the *New Review of Books and Religion*, founder and editor of *Brownies' Book*, and of *Phylon*, a journal in race relations published quarterly by Atlanta University. DuBois was instrumental in undertaking the publication of an encyclopedia of black Americans. Based on his writings, DuBois gave thousands of addresses in colleges, universities, churches, and public halls in the United States and throughout the world, including Great Britain, China, the Soviet Union, Haiti, Japan, and Cuba.[14]

DuBois served as secretary for the first Pan-African Conference in England and was the chief organizer of the Modern Pan-African Movement. He was among the original founders of the National Association for the Advancement of Colored People and was the founder and general secretary of the Niagara Movement.

Chapter II
Mordecai Wyatt Johnson (1890–1976)
Minister, Orator, Educator

What were the social, political, economic, and educational conditions for blacks in America when Mordecai Wyatt Johnson was born January 12, 1890, in Paris, Tennessee? Opportunities at that time were deplorable in every respect; blacks were not far removed from the yoke of physical slavery and oppression. They were forced to live in segregation and to function as second-class citizens. In many instances, they had to build their own institutions of higher learning without adequate financial support from the government. Whites said to blacks that they must pull themselves up by their bootstraps; but blacks had none to pull, and whites did nothing to assist them in obtaining any. Blacks were systematically consigned to economic, cultural, social, and educational death. Many whites were programmed toward a negative view of blacks as an inferior people.[1]

Because of the difficult pressures, many blacks succumbed to the philosophy of accommodation and gradualism in order to survive. The chief exponent of this strand of thought was Booker T. Washington, who blamed blacks for their own predicament and contended that whites were their best friends. Washington accepted the separate but equal doctrine, verbally minimized the extent of racism in America, and advised blacks against political activism.

He argued for industrial education, as opposed to higher education, as being their most viable direction.[2] Mordecai Johnson emerged as a major force in changing the social, educational, political, religious, and economic conditions that Booker T. Washington had helped to create for blacks in America.

Early Life and Development

Mordecai Johnson was raised in a religious atmosphere. His father's pastorate of Mt. Zion Baptist Church in Paris laid the foundation for Mordecai's interest in the ministry. He attended Howe Institute in Memphis, and later enrolled in Atlanta Baptist College (later named Morehouse College) at the age of sixteen, graduating with honors in 1911. He received the bachelor's degree from the University of Chicago in 1913. After being divinely led to the ministry, Johnson decided to attend theological seminary. He was convinced that the black church needed educated black clergy in order to maintain its historic mission toward freedom and liberation of the oppressed. He received the Bachelor of Divinity degree from the then Rochester Theological Seminary and the Master of Sacred Theology from Harvard Divinity School.

He made the observation in his inaugural address as president of Howard University, June 10, 1927, that "there are forty-seven thousand Negro churches in the United States and there are in the whole country today less than sixty college graduates getting ready to fill these pulpits." He perceived this lack of educated clergy as tragic; he firmly believed that the black church, from every point of view, is the most powerful and constructive organization now at work in the black community. "There is no organization and no combination of organizations which can, at this stage in the history of the Negro race, begin to compare with the fundamental importance of the Negro

Church."[3] In order to maintain this importance, Johnson felt it was essential to produce well-educated black ministers.

Theology

Faith and Eschatology

What accounts for the survival of black Americans, in spite of oppression, slavery, second-class citizenship, and racism? Why didn't they perish in slavery? And what does the future hold? These questions reach the core of Johnson's understanding of faith and eschatology. He first grounded his faith in the historic struggle, pain, and prayer of black Americans and their flight toward freedom and liberation. He categorized this as "The Faith of the American Negro." Based on this historic faith, he anchored himself to the eschatological future. Eschatology, as traditionally used in theology, refers to the "last things," human destiny, or the ultimate fate of humanity. Johnson reinterpreted it in light of the future of blacks in America in regard to political, educational, economic, cultural, and social conditions. His emphases were not on the traditional notion of "pie in the sky by and by" or "when we get over yonder, everything will be all right" kind of theology. Rather, his emphases were geared toward the actualization of peace, brotherhood, love, justice, and liberation here in America.

Johnson's faith, as he interlocked it with that of black Americans historically, was based on belief in the love and providence of a just and holy God, belief in the principles of democracy and the righteous purpose of the federal government, and belief in the ultimate disposition of the country. But why did he believe in America? He had every reason to doubt. After slavery, it had said to black Americans, "Find your place of inferiority and stay in it." "Act like black Americans should act," said the mass media, "Work like blacks should work, and talk like blacks should talk." America made every attempt to erase from the minds of black Americans all visions of the achievement of independence and self-respect. It made every effort to force blacks to realize the necessity of "keeping their place" in society. Collective attacks against the property of blacks were perpetrated; blacks were lynched, and the lynchings were advertised with photographs of dead bodies.[4] In spite of all this, Johnson maintained faith in America. Why?

In the first place, he held the firm conviction that truth was at the center of the cosmos—that is, that the orderly universe ultimately bends toward justice, goodness, love, and mercy. Because of this, Johnson was able to look beyond the cruelty of black suffering toward an eschatological future of genuine freedom and liberation in this world. He referred to this when he said, "I do not conceal my hope, that this destiny will be entire public equality and entire good-willed cooperative relations with every element of the American population, and that he will be especially understood by those men who have been his former masters and who have been accustomed to make him a slave."[5] Johnson thought America could conquer all the inhibitions associated with blackness and create an environment where blacks and whites could exist interdependently, without opposition.

Education and Freedom

The theological training that Johnson received at home, and his education at Rochester Theological Seminary and Harvard greatly contributed to his enlarged vision and his approach to education and freedom. In fact, he undergirded his philosophy with theological presuppositions. His firm belief in the inherent dignity and freedom of the individual compelled him to challenge blacks to rise above their immediate environment intellectually and strive for success. Johnson realized that the industrial educational philosophy of Booker T. Washington was fast becoming of little value, and upon his appointment as the first black president of Howard University, he perceived the need to develop studies in sociology, economics, history, social philosophy, biology, and anthropology. He knew, at this point, that he was going against the grain of the dominant American opinion in regard to higher education for blacks—that blacks are inherently incapable of critical thinking or of mastering basic academic disciplines.[6] In spite of the opposition to and the controversies over his untiring efforts to advance Howard University toward higher levels of educational pursuits, Johnson had deep confidence that such studies were essential. He said, "If the Negro studies the human will, human motive, human organization, the philosophy of social life, in order to discover how he may become free, with the consent of the other elements of the American population, he is sure to discover something about the human will, something about human motives and human organization that may be to the advantage of mankind."[7]

Johnson viewed education as an essential prerequisite for freedom. He knew that blacks could not function within society, nor could they experience genuine freedom without an adequate education. He knew that they could not properly interpret their constitutional rights or adapt to new trends in society. This lack would result in a new form of slavery. In other words, Johnson knew that blacks had to learn how to function within the socio-economic, political, and cultural system in which they found themselves. The aim of his philosophy of education, in an effort to lead black Americans toward complete freedom, was to produce among blacks of Howard University self-consciousness, self-direction, independence, and responsibility. He wanted to impart knowledge of proper conduct, knowledge of their past and present, and the ability to project the future, as well as the courage to speak out and to act in behalf of justice.

Johnson felt that only the application of persistent intellect, in a multiplicity of complex directions, with one goal in mind, offered the possibility of attaining complete freedom and justice for black Americans. With such a goal in mind, Johnson believed that America needed Howard University, where intellectual pursuits would be undertaken in a comprehensive manner, enabling not only black Americans but the entire nation to understand the black situation, where blacks want to go, what the difficulties are, and how, in spite of these difficulties, blacks can achieve their goals by the proper application of intellect.

Contribution

The election of Mordecai Wyatt Johnson to the presidency of Howard University in 1926 was viewed by many as a giant step toward freedom for black Americans. Newspapers throughout the country hailed the appointment as one of the most significant events in the history of the university. Howard was referred to as "the capstone of Negro education," and Mordecai Johnson was soon to bring about a renaissance in its scholastic direction.

In an effort to achieve the aims of his philosophy of education, Johnson realized the need to attract and develop a distinguished teaching staff, contending that an educational institution is no greater than its faculty. He felt that men and women who must worry every night about whether they can pay their bills are not free to develop self-consciousness, self-respect, responsibility, independence, courage, and confidence in their students. He reported in 1926 that the highest salary for a professor at Howard University was $2,650—a salary below those paid in the public high school system in the city of Washington. He indicated further that there were teachers at Howard earning only $1,000 to $1,400 per year. Johnson then asked how Howard could achieve its aims, with teachers making such low wages. These conditions had a bad effect, not only on the faculty, but also on the students, the products of the institution. He pointed out that "poorly paid teachers who must work in the night to supplement their salaries, preaching and selling—even coffins—as some of them have done and are doing, will find it impossible to turn out anything other than a mass product."[8] He knew that mass production in industry may be a desirable thing, but in education, to a large degree, it is achieved at the expense of quality. Therefore, he strove to make the salaries at Howard competitive with those of other universities its size. The July 17, 1978, issue of the *Chronicle of Higher Education* reported the salary, including fringe benefits, of a professor at Howard University to be $32,700. Of course, this is to be credited to the present president, James Cheek; but it is important to note that Mordecai Johnson laid the foundation during his thirty-four-year tenure as president of Howard.

In 1928, Johnson led Congress to amend the charter of Howard University, thereby authorizing annual appropriations. Twenty major buildings were constructed while he was at Howard, the capital assets of the university tripled, the number of volumes in the libraries doubled, and fulltime faculty increased by 98.7 percent.[9] Many distinguished scholars were attracted, and Howard University became internationally known, with an outstanding reputation.

Johnson accomplished many things at Howard, but his philosophy of education stands above all else. He insisted that the purpose of education is not only to free persons' minds, but also to lift them from second-class citizenship, poverty, oppression, and suffering. He viewed Howard University as the center for such educational endeavors.

Mordecai Johnson was a person of extraordinary intellectual ability. He distinguished himself as an educator, scholar, orator, theologian, civil rights worker, and humanitarian. He lectured throughout America and the world on issues related to the flight of black Americans toward freedom, influencing thousands of men and women in all walks of life and of all ethnic backgrounds.

In 1950, he returned from a visit to India. At that time, Martin Luther King, Jr. was a student at Crozer Theological Seminary in Pennsylvania. One Sunday afternoon, Johnson lectured at the Fellowship House in Philadelphia, and King was in the audience. Johnson maintained in his address that the nonviolent philosophy used by Ghandi in India was applicable to the race problem in America. Stirred by these words, King purchased a half-dozen books on Ghandi's life and thought.[10] King didn't realize at the time that this philosophy was the weapon he would use to shake the foundations of racism, segregation, poverty, and man's inhumanity to man in America.

Chapter III
Benjamin Elijah Mays (1895–   )
Sociologist of Religion,
Minister, Educator

Early Life and Development

The parents of Benjamin Elijah Mays were born into slavery. His father, Hezekiah Mays, was born in 1856 and his mother, Louvenia Carter Mays, in 1862. His mother could neither read nor write and his father could read very little. Benjamin Elijah was born on August 1, 1894, in the little town of Ninety-Six, South Carolina, fourteen miles from the county seat of Greenwood.

It was a critical period in the politics of South Carolina. The decline of black participation in politics came to a culmination in 1895, when the Constitutional Convention of that state made it illegal for blacks to vote. Benjamin Mays grew up in a world where he and all other blacks were completely disfranchised. Shortly after 1900, legal disfranchisement of blacks throughout the South was complete. The state of Mississippi led the way in 1890, with South Carolina following in 1895. Louisiana disfranchised blacks in 1898, North Carolina in 1900, and Virginia, Georgia, Florida, Tennessee, and other southern states followed in one manner or another. Benjamin Mays was unable to vote until 1946, when the white primary in Georgia was declared unconstitutional; at that time he was serving as president of Morehouse College in Atlanta.

BENJAMIN ELIJAH MAYS (1895–   )

Not only did Mays experience disfranchisement, but he also lived in a climate where it was common for blacks to be lynched, black women were raped at will by white men, and whites frequently perpetrated mob violence against blacks. When an issue developed between a black and a white, the courts invariably ruled in favor of the white, and discrimination and inequality in education were taken for granted. Countless books and articles were published, sermons were preached, and public lectures were given, with one theme: The Negro is a different breed. He is inferior to the white man. At any cost he must be kept down.

When Benjamin Mays was not yet five years old, a crowd of white men on horseback and carrying rifles degraded his father with foul language, drew their weapons, and forced him to salute, take off his hat, and bow down to them several times. The memory of that experience stayed with Benjamin Mays. The mob did not stop with the degradation of his father; that incident was only a part of the Phoenix riot, which started in Greenwood County, South Carolina, on November 8, 1898, and brought fear and terror to blacks throughout the South. Blacks were lynched and beaten at random. Mays was four years old when the Phoenix riot occurred. He was twelve at the time of the Atlanta riot.[1]

Early in life, Mays realized the odds were stacked against him. Growing up at a time when blacks were consigned to social, cultural, political, economic, and educational inferiority created frustrations and doubts in his mind. He realized he lived in a white man's world—a world of white supremacy and control. He asked, "How can I be free in this world? How can I grow to my full stature as a man?" The white child born in 1894 in South Carolina knew that the county, the town, the state, and the nation belonged to whites and therefore to him. But as one of the disinherited black children of his day, Mays asked, "How can I know that a part of the nation, the state, and the county belongs to me too?" How could he exist without cringing and kowtowing to whites? How could he walk the earth with dignity and pride? How could he become inspired to achieve, to accomplish, and to "be somebody," when everything in his environment negated his existence? He answers, "Although I can appreciate the current emphasis on blackness, I am mighty glad I didn't have to wait seventy years for someone in the late 1960s to teach me to appreciate what I am—black! Many times my mother, unlettered and untutored though she was, said to us children, 'You are as good as anybody!' "[2]

Although the white world did not accept the philosophy of his mother, that philosophy served as a basic source of encouragement and support for Mays. Within his home, pictures of Frederick Douglas, Booker T. Washington, and Paul Lawrence Dunbar hung on the walls. Mays has said that in his high school days, Booker T. Washington meant more to him than George Washington; Frederick Douglas meant more than William Lloyd Garrison; and Paul Lawrence Dunbar inspired him more than Longfellow. Therefore, in spite of living in a world of white supremacy and stereotypical notions of black inferiority, Mays soon found his identity, and he was determined to succeed and make a contribution to humanity. This determination began to realize itself when he graduated as valedictorian from high school in Orangeburg, South Carolina, in 1916, earned the B.A. degree with honors from Bates College, Lewiston, Maine, in 1920, and received the M.A. and Ph.D. degrees from the University of Chicago in 1925 and 1935, respectively.

Theology

The Black Church

One of the factors that contributed significantly to the breadth of his accomplishments is the fact that Mays discovered his identity very early in life. He knew who he was, where he had come from, and where he was going, in spite of many obstacles. Where did the masses of blacks find their identity? The answer to this question takes us into a discussion of Mays' conception of the black church.

In the summer of 1930, a Rockefeller-financed organization, the Institute of Social and Religious Research, invited Mays to direct a comprehensive study of the black church in the United States. Mays, along with Joseph W. Nicholson, a Colored Methodist Episcopal minister, began the study of 691 black churches in twelve cities: Atlanta, Baltimore, Birmingham, Charleston, Chicago, Cincinnati, Detroit, Houston, Memphis, New Orleans, Philadelphia, and Richmond. They also studied 185 rural black churches. What significance has the black church had for blacks historically, and what significance does it continue to have today?

The study of Mays and Nicholson revealed that the black church has been a source of identity for blacks. They discovered that the opportunity found in the black church to be recognized as somebody of value and dignity, and to possess a position of importance, has stimulated pride and preserved self-respect in blacks who otherwise would have been entirely beaten and completely submerged by their existence. Both socially and psychologically, every person has a need for recognition and importance. Historically, the black church has supplied this need. A truck driver can become the chairman of the deacon board. A janitor or a waitress can become the superintendent of the Sunday school. A woman who has no social status becomes head of the missionary society. The boy or girl with little training can become a leading voice in the church choir. These people receive very little recognition in their daily jobs, and society doesn't give them the needed feeling of worth. Very often their souls are crushed and their personalities are not noticed. But in the black church, they are given status, recognition, value, dignity, and a purpose for living.[3]

According to Mays and Nicholson, the black church was the first community or public organization to be owned and completely controlled by blacks. Further, they pointed out, the black church provides an opportunity for freedom, self-expression, and release from the restriction of obstacles faced daily by blacks. When blacks were segregated from public and privately owned institutions and amusement places, they resorted to the black church. The church took the place of theaters, dance halls, and other places of recreation; suppers, lectures, recitals, debates, and plays were held regularly. Throughout its existence, the black church has also encouraged black participation in higher education, business, politics, economic growth and development, and social cohesion and cultural stability.[4]

Mays emphasizes that today, many are inclined to downplay the influence of the black church on education. He said, "I hardly know what I might have become were it not for the encouragement that unlettered church people gave me when I was a frustrated youth handering for an education. They were mostly illiterate, but intelligent. They said to me: Keep on, Bennie, you will overcome someday."[5]

What is required of the present black church? Beyond worship, fellowship, support of civil rights, consolation of the bereaved, burial of the dead, marriage of the young, and interpretation of the prophetic gospel, what are some of the demands? Mays challenges the church when he points out that the dropout rate in the public school system is higher among blacks than it is among whites. These dropouts are likely to become criminals or dope addicts. Mays feels that the church cannot afford to leave this challenge wholly to the schools. What can the black church do? "Each major church could adopt one or more middle schools or one or more high schools and in cooperation with the schools work out a program designed to prevent dropping out or to encourage the dropout to continue his education in some way."[6]

Another critical area today is the homicide rate among blacks, which is much higher than among whites. It is the responsibility of the black church to develop programs within the black community to reduce that rate. Mays argues that "if the black church doesn't do it, it will hardly be done. We should not expect the white church to do what is primarily the responsibility of the black church."[7] Other critical areas facing the black church today are, according to Mays, unemployment and poverty, suicide, alcoholism, crime, and divorce.

Idea of God

The concept of God as reflected in the thought of Mays did not develop from philosophical and theological debate, nor did it originate from his academic studies at Bates College and the University of Chicago, although those studies did lead to a systematic and refined formulation of that concept. His approach to God grew first from his mother's religious influence. She taught him to pray and trust in God, and she influenced him frequently in his prayer and search. Mays was not as optimistic as his mother, but many nights as a boy, when he worked alone in the field by moonlight, his search for God compelled him to hitch the mule to a tree and go down into the woods to pray. He said, "My prayers were all variations of the same theme: a petition to God to enable me to get away to school. My desire for an education was not only a dream but a goal that drove me and prodded me, day and night."[8]

His quest for God reached both a subjective and an objective refinement and formulation with the publication in 1938 of The Negro's God. Reflecting on the many difficult experiences in his own life and considering events since 1760, he perceived that the reality of God played a dominant role in the survival of black Americans. In his study, Mays sought to interpret the reality of God in classical literature from 1760 to the twentieth century, as reflected in the thought of black Americans. His contention is that this literature reveals ideas of God adhering to compensatory patterns, ideas of God centered around social activism, and ideas of God involving doubt, agnosticism, and atheism.[9] The reality of God as conceived by Mays focuses around social activism. He sees God as a moving dynamic reality, facilitating the flight of blacks and other oppressed people toward social justice and goodness.

For Mays, the reality of God represents optimism over pessimism. This optimism, he feels, must say to every black child that the sky is the limit—not the ceiling, but the sky. It means that all things are possible for those who love God and work to accomplish something worthwhile. Mays contends that the reality of God is that he has no hands but our hands, no legs but our legs, and no conscience except ours to prod us to achieve our goals. Mays' whole life is a testimony to the integration of the reality of God into a constructive social activism that will bring freedom for black Americans.[10]

Doctrine of Man

Mays accepts the biblical notion of the creation of man—that God breathed into man's nostrils the breath of life, and that man became a living soul. The thing, therefore, that distinguishes man from all other creatures, according to Mays, is the image of God in man. Every person was created by God to do something special, something unique, something worthwhile; and if that person doesn't do it, it will not be done. During his life, Mays has developed a growing pessimism about man, based on empirical reality—the contradictory nature of man. In creating man, God faced a dilemma—whether to make man free with potential for good and evil or to make him a robot without the capacity to know right from wrong. "So in making man free to choose, [God] had to make him free to choose right or wrong, truth or falsehood, peace or war, the high road or the low road."[11] In reference to this contradiction, Mays aligns himself with the theologian Paul Tillich, who argues that only he who is made in the image of God (meaning man) has the capacity to separate himself from God. In this regard, the greatness and weakness of man are identical. And even God himself cannot remove man's greatness without destroying his weakness. However, if man had not received this contradictory nature, he would have been merely a thing among things and unable to glorify the divine majesty of God.[12]

Because of this paradoxical nature, Mays is sensitive to the fact that man is potentially both honest and dishonest, forgiving and vengeful, trustworthy and deceitful, capable of rising to the heights and descending to the depths, and capable of building a kingdom of either heaven or hell on earth. Which direction will man take?

Mays' pessimism about man is heightened because he realizes that increased mental capacity cannot influence the heart. There is no necessary correlation between increased knowledge and increased goodness. Socrates felt there was such a correlation. His contention was that ignorance is equivalent to sin—that a person does evil things because of ignorance. Socrates believed that if a person knows what is good, then he will do what is good. Mays argues to the contrary, "We know now that knowledge is not enough; that man can know the truth and deliberately walk in darkness, see the 'high road' beckoning to him and deliberately choose the 'low road.' "[13]

Mays, however, transcends his pessimistic view in saying that, although there is a contradiction in the nature of man, there is an element of divinity in him that will never disappear. When man reduces himself to his worst state and finds himself in the gutter of iniquity, the element of divinity in him rises up and makes him ashamed. Although man may not be able to overcome his sinful tendencies, deep within his soul he wants to be decent. Because of the image of God in man, man cannot leave God, and God cannot leave man. They are interwoven. Someday, the hope is that man will realize that the ways of God are just and righteous, and that by obeying God, the earth will become a place of love, brotherhood, justice, peace, and goodwill.[14]

Faith and Righteousness

A firm belief in God and in human potential, along with a profound commitment to righteousness, has played a dominant role in the life and legacy of Benjamin E. Mays. His life testifies to this abiding and conquering faith. For Mays, faith is not a blind chance, ignorance, a leap in the dark; neither is it the opposite of reasoning or the rejection of scientific fact. Faith, Mays argues, is partial understanding and courage to take the next step. It is a commitment to something noble and worthwhile. "Faith is belief in an ideal that you know is real but which you also know will never be attained. Faith is a belief that, however rocky the road, however thorny the path, tomorrow things will be better."[15] What then is faith? It is taking a giant step and putting the consequences in the hands of God.

Faith is the inner urge, the inner compulsion, the drive that one possesses to accomplish a goal. It is this inner drive that has enabled Mays to succeed in spite of the obstacles of racism, oppression, and second-class citizenship. But does this cause him to boast? Does he feel that his success gave him special favors in the sight of God?

Mays is critical of the better-than-thou attitude. He sees righteousness as a gift from God, and not as a state which can be earned. He contends that one who understands life and the frailty of all mankind never lifts himself above others, never attempts to extricate himself from the masses. The righteousness of God makes the individual want to identify with the masses, because he realizes he is both a part of, and involved with, mankind. Faith and righteousness enable a person to help others. Mays indicates this when he says, "You cannot help a man if you think you are better than he is. A man may be poor, but don't look down on him. He may be ignorant, but don't take his dignity."[16]

Contribution

The contributions of Benjamin Elijah Mays are too numerous to mention in a few pages. His recent autobiography bears an appropriate title, *Born to Rebel*; his entire life has been centered around protest against the social evils that seek to keep black Americans oppressed. In his introduction to *Born to Rebel*, one of Mays' former students, Samuel Cook, at one time a professor of political science at Atlanta and Duke universities, and now president of Dillard University in New Orleans, commented that if racism were not so cancerous within America, Mays might have devoted more time to ultimate philosophical and religious issues. Cook wrote that Mays, because of his seminal intellect and inexhaustible energy, is a potential Paul Tillich, Reinhold Niebuhr, Karl Barth, Rudolf Bultmann, Martin Buber, Emil Brunner, or Walter Rauschenbusch.[17]

Although the assessment Cook made is well deserved, it does not adequately depict the magnitude of Mays' capacity to synthesize philosophical and theological theory with social reality. While living a life of social activism, Mays has been very productive as a theologian. He is the author of seven books and more than one hundred articles. He has written numerous newspaper pieces and scholarly chapters in more than fifteen books. Most of his writings deal with deep theological issues and their application to race relations within the context of America and of the world. He has refused to allow his social activism to keep him away from the constant intellectual rigor of genuine scholarship.

Mays' involvement in ministry, higher education, politics, and the issues of world peace and race relations has made him one of the most sought-after speakers in America. He has delivered major addresses to over 250 colleges, universities, and public schools, and has been guest preacher and speaker at more than five hundred churches. Because of his many pioneering contributions to higher education, race relations, and to humanity in general, Mays has received more than forty-two honorary doctorates from leading institutions both in America and in other nations. Additionally, he is the recipient of at least 210 awards.

Among the many positions held throughout his life, one of his major appointments was as dean of the School of Religion at Howard University. Upon the invitation of Mordecai Wyatt Johnson, Mays accepted that appointment in 1934. When he became dean, several urgent needs immediately came to his attention: to increase the enrollment; to upgrade the quality of the faculty; to improve the physical plant; to enlarge the library building and increase the number of volumes; to develop an endowment; and to seek accreditation by the American Association of Theological Schools. In his six years at Howard, four of these concerns were accomplished: an enlarged graduate enrollment was made a reality; the faculty was strengthened; the library was enlarged; and the School of Religion was accredited.

In 1940, Mays was invited to become president of Morehouse College in Atlanta. It was there that he became internationally known and respected as a distinguished educator, minister, lecturer, statesman, humanitarian, advocate of civil rights, and authority on race relations in America. Under his strong leadership, Morehouse College became one of the outstanding black institutions of higher learning, with full membership in the Southern Association of Colleges and Schools. He served as president for twenty-seven years, retiring in 1967.

During his tenure at Morehouse, Mays influenced the lives of thousands of young men toward achievement of academic excellence and moral character, opposition to all forms of discrimination, and success in the outside world. Each student was made to realize that wherever he went and whatever he did in life, he represented Morehouse College. To be a Morehouse man was a mark of distinction, pride, and intellectual excellence. Morehouse men were known for their courage, dedication to scholarship, and determination to succeed in life in spite of the forces of racism and oppression. Because of these high standards, Morehouse men serve in important positions throughout the world. Many are professors, physicians, lawyers, dentists, ministers, engineers, college presidents and deans, editors, and authors.

Mays has continued to serve humanity since his retirement. In 1969, he was elected to the Atlanta Board of Education and has since been reelected as a member and as president, on several occasions.

Chapter IV
Howard Thurman (1900–   )
Minister, Orator, Theologian, Educator

There is not one category adequate to describe the depth and span of the life and thought of Howard Thurman. He is an outstanding philosopher, theologian, orator, preacher, poet, mystic, and humanitarian. He was named by *Life* magazine in the April 6, 1953, edition as one of twelve great preachers of the twentieth century. Further attesting to the magnitude of Thurman's oratorical ability, he has lectured to faculty and students in more than five hundred institutions around the world. These lecture tours have exposed the ideas of Thurman to some of the finest scholars in the world today, who in turn have contributed significantly to the depth and comprehensiveness of his thought.

Early Life and Development

Thurman was born November 18, 1900, in Daytona Beach, Florida. He entered Morehouse College in 1919, after attending Florida Normal and Industrial Institute. During Thurman's student days at Morehouse, Benjamin Mays was a member of the faculty. Mays has said that Thurman was one of the most brilliant students he had encountered during his years of teaching. Mays points to

Thurman as living proof that God calls persons from all races and ethnic groups to do his mighty works, and that genius is no respecter of persons. It springs from all classes and races, high and low, great and small, rich and poor.[1] Mays and Thurman developed a friendship at Morehouse College that has lasted through the years.

In 1922, during his senior year, Thurman applied for admission to Newton Theological Seminary in Massachusetts, to study for the ministry. His application was rejected, because at that time Newton did not admit blacks as students. Thurman reports, "In the letter which was sent to me, it was suggested that I should seek entrance to Virginia Union University (a Negro institution) where I could be trained in the kind of leadership that I would need in order to serve my own people."[2]

Thurman rose above this direct instance of discrimination and made application to Colgate-Rochester Seminary, where he later graduated with the Bachelor of Divinity degree. He did additional study with the Quaker philosopher, Rufus Jones, of Haverford College.

Because of Thurman's profound creative theological insights and his electrifying and penetrating oratory, he has attracted countless followers from all walks of life and of all races. Serving as dean of Marsh Chapel at Boston University from 1953 to 1964, he attracted large audiences at the chapel services on Sunday morning both from within and outside the university. In this capacity he touched and greatly influenced the lives of thousands of students, faculty, and laypersons. He did not confine himself to the pulpit during his days at Boston University, but also won respect throughout the university as an effective teacher in the School of Theology. In recognition of his many distinguished years of service to the university, he was made dean emeritus, Marsh Chapel, Boston University, in 1965. Prior to going to Boston, Thurman had already left a great legacy at Howard University, where he served as dean of Rankin Chapel and professor of theology.

Theology

The Unity of Life

Unity of life is a theme that flows through the bulk of Howard Thurman's writings. It is central to his life and thought. By unity, he means that life in its totality is interrelated and interdependent. Unity of life is a metaphysical principle for Thurman; not only does it describe life itself, but it is also at the heart of existence. Without this basic truth, philosophers, theologians, sociologists, psychologists, mathematicians, physicists, chemists, and others would be unable to function. The principle of unity and order is the basic foundation; everything in existence was made possible originally at creation and continues because of the principle of unity. The creative process moved from chaos, disorganization, and disunity into order, harmony, and unity.

Based on this metaphysical principle, Thurman argues that the background of man's existence is community. He feels that a person is threatened by a sense of isolation when he is cut off from his fellows. Although a person may try, he cannot completely succeed in isolating himself, for mutual interdependence is characteristic of the totality of life. If the individual, however, insists on cutting himself away from the nourishment of other individuals, or from particular individuals, Thurman contends that the result is a wasting away, a starvation, a failure of that life to be sustained.

Is the desire to be nourished, to function in community, characteristic of all life? Thurman says it is a built-in urge, an ingredient of life in its simplest and most configurated dimensions. But although the creative urge or tendency in life is toward community, it can or may decide to move into chaos and disunity. Each expression of life contains community as a possibility or potentiality. "The degree to which the potential in any expression of life is actualized marks the extent to which such an expression of life

48

experiences wholeness, integration, community."[3] Where does one find the clue to community? Thurman says it can be found in the inner creative activity of living creatures. For example, as cells and organisms realize themselves, they experience adaptability and integration into the whole.

The religious basis of Thurman's understanding of community is the affirmation that the Mind of God actualizes itself in time. This means that there are observable patterns in all creation. "From this point of view, all time-space manifestations of substance—in short, all things, even existence itself—are regarded as the Mind of God coming to itself in time and space."[4] Thurman contends that both history and nature support this truth. If this is so, then what is existence? Thurman responds that it is divine activity. It follows that if the Mind of God manifests itself throughout all life, the principle of rationality is at the heart of existence, and this rationality accounts for order in life.

Seeing life in the context of community, how does Thurman then account for man's experience of oppression, social malfunctions, sin, and other evils that work against community? Is Thurman referring to community in the abstract? Or does his understanding of community include both the ideal and the concrete? Thurman distinguishes between man's experience of community as an actuality and the ideal community as potential. The beginning point of the human on earth was that of order, wholeness, and integration. This for Thurman is the ideal community, and its background should form the basis for community as potential. Originally, man was innocent, but his first decision triggered disharmony, and he was no longer innocent. "Man's original experience of community is both potential and actualized potential within the framework of innocence."[5] Presently, man has the capacity to experience either community or chaos.

Christian Hope

As a Christian theologian, Thurman bases his notion of Christian hope in the reality of the Resurrection. He sees continuity between the reality of the Resurrection and the creative urge of life itself to move toward a synthesis, a growing together, and an integration into a community, in spite of its contradictions. Christian hope, therefore, is based on what Thurman refers to as the growing edge.

Thurman contends that we see this growing edge present in nature. Within the heart of the dying plant, it seems that vitality is present. On an oak tree, the leaves turn yellow and die, but they remain present on the tree throughout the winter. Why is this the case? During the winter, the business of the tree is to hold on to the dead leaves; when a change takes place within the heart of the tree, life moves to another dimension, the tree no longer holds on to the leaves, and in their place, buds emerge. Thurman's point is simply that no expression of life exhausts any aspect of life.

One of the most penetrating insights into Thurman's understanding of Christian hope is to be found in his interpretation of Negro spirituals. His two volumes on the subject, *The Negro Spiritual Speaks of Life and Death* (given at Harvard University in 1947 as the Ingersoll Lectures on the immortality of man) and *Deep River* remain classics today in the annals of black religious thought. The clue to his understanding of Christian hope is present in his explanation of the Negro spiritual, "There Is a Balm in Gilead."

> There is a balm in Gilead,
> To make the spirit whole.
> There is a balm in Gilead,
> To heal the sin-sick soul.

In his discussion of this spiritual, Thurman described it within the context of the book of Jeremiah. Because of difficult circumstances, the prophet Jeremiah found himself spiritually depressed and tortured. As a result, he asked, "Is there no balm in Gilead; is there no physician there?" (Jer. 8:22). These questions depict Jeremiah's search within his own soul as he was stripped to the literal substance of himself and pushed by vicissitudes to the core of his existence. His feeling was that "there must be a balm in Gilead; it cannot be that there is no balm in Gilead."[6]

Thurman argued that enslaved black Americans caught the mood of this spiritual dilemma, straightened the question mark in Jeremiah's statement into an exclamation point, and said, "There is a balm in Gilead!" In this example of Christian hope, the basic insight is an optimism that grows out of the pessimism of life; it uses the pessimism of life as raw material, transcends it, and creates its own strength. The background of this optimism, according to Thurman, is that life has its own restraint, and that there is a moral order to which the life of each individual is bound.

The basis of this moral order is the belief that the contradictions of life are in themselves neither final nor ultimate. Thurman felt this is the basic difference between optimism and pessimism. The pessimist assesses the facts of experience and on their face value makes a final judgment. "Back of such a view is the conception that life in essence is fixed, finished, unchanging. Man is caught in the agonizing grip of inevitables; and whatever may be his chance or circumstantial assignment, all his alternatives are reduced to zero."[7] But on the other hand, Thurman argued, if perchance the contradictions of life are not ultimate, there is always the growing edge of hope in the most difficult, challenging, and tragic situations. This is the basis of Christian hope, and it is grounded in the conviction that the ultimate destiny of man is good.

Thurman's philosophy of Christian hope goes against all notions of social superiority and racial inequality. He was quite aware of those philosophies arguing that the God of the universe is partial, immoral, or amoral, and that he has consigned selected persons or races to be superior over others. But because of a philosophy of hope based on the conviction that the contradictions of life ultimately exhaust themselves, Thurman contended, "We continue to hope against all evidence to the contrary, because that hope is fed by a conviction deeper than the processes of thought that the destiny of man is good."[8]

Jesus Christ

In *Jesus and the Disinherited*, published in 1949, Thurman provided a penetrating interpretation of Jesus, with a focus on those persons in history who have had their backs against the wall. Is there a normative interpretation of Jesus that is acceptable? Or is there a standard interpretation of Jesus that generally appeals to most people? Thurman said the standard interpretation of Jesus is developed by those who stand at the top looking down; as a result, their interpretation doesn't speak significantly to those who are at the bottom looking up. Does this mean then that traditional interpretations of the life and thought of Jesus have been toward the perpetuation of those at the top? Thurman answered, "Many and varied are the interpretations dealing with the teachings and the life of Jesus of Nazareth. But few of these interpretations deal with what the teachings and the life of Jesus have to say to those who stand, at a moment in human history, with their backs against the wall."[9] Thurman was acutely aware that the majority of people live with their backs against the wall; they are the poor, the dispossessed, the disinherited. The fundamental question of modern times, therefore, is, What does Christianity have to say to these people?

Thurman began his interpretation with the recognition of Jesus' ancestry—Jesus was a Jew. To understand Jesus, he argued, one must recognize that he must be perceived within the context of the sense of community that Israel held with God. The second point Thurman made is that Jesus was a poor Jew. The economic status of Jesus placed him with the great masses of people on earth, for the masses of people on earth are poor. The third point is that Jesus was a member of a minority group in the midst of a larger dominant and controlling group.

What does Jesus have to say to those with their backs against the wall? Thurman stated that Jesus says to this generation the same things he said to his own generation, that "anyone who permits another to determine the quality of his inner life gives into the hands of the other the keys to his destiny."[10] An individual may be forced to submit under physical oppression or force. In such a situation, the individual could resist and protest the submission but ultimately find himself coerced into it. One's outer self can be controlled by coercion, but the individual is not destroyed until he submits his inner self. It is the inner self that must never be submitted. The inner self enables the individual to rise above the immediate situation, regardless of how tragic, and to work toward its eradication. This is the message, Thurman said, that Jesus brought to his generation; he brings the same message to those in this generation who have their backs against the wall.

Contribution

The contributions of Howard Thurman to humanity have been varied, vast, and significant. His ideas have influenced thousands of college students, laypersons, ministers, and scholars. He has always been able to communicate with the common man who has no formal training, as well as with the most advanced scholars. In spite of his many outstanding accomplishments and successful ventures, Thurman has always maintained the common touch.

Having retired from a distinguished career as minister-at-large, dean of Marsh Chapel, and professor of spiritual resources and disciplines at Boston University, Thurman lives in San Francisco with his wife, the former Sue Bailey, who is an author and social historian. The Thurmans have two daughters, Olive Wong, a librarian and playwright in New York, and Anne Chiarenza, who is a journalist and an attorney.

Thurman has organized the Howard Thurman Educational Trust Foundation in San Francisco, which contains all his sermons, lectures, meditation cassettes, books and other publications. The purpose of this trust corporation is to provide a channel to acquire and disburse funds for the support of religious, charitable, scientific, literary, and educational causes. Each year, hundreds of ministers, scholars, and laypersons come to the foundation for counseling and to learn more about Thurman's ideas.

Thurman is a fellow of the American Academy of Arts and Sciences. He serves on the board of trustees of Boston University and is a member of the National Council of Religion in Higher Education. On two occasions he was chosen narrator for the rendition of Honneger's oratorio "King David," performed by the San Francisco Symphony Orchestra and the San Francisco Municipal Chorus. He was also chosen as guest narrator for the presentation of the oratorio "Esther," written by the contemporary composer, March Laviz, especially for the centennial celebration of Temple Beth Israel in San Francisco,

In recognition of his many outstanding contributions to humanity, in 1976 the British Broadcasting Corporation produced the documentary film, *The Life and Thought of Howard Thurman.*

Chapter V
Adam Clayton Powell, Jr. (1908–1972)
Minister, Politician

Early Life and Development

Many sociologists, anthropologists, and psychologists argue that a strong family background is essential in the socialization and acculturation process. Adam Clayton Powell, Jr., grew up in one such strong household, which nurtured and prepared him to emerge at the proper time, in his own right, as an outstanding preacher, politician, educator, orator, civil rights leader, and spokesman for human dignity. Powell was instructed by his parents in such areas as race, politics, economics, and religion, and the values received from this instruction remained with him throughout his life.

Adam Clayton Powell, Jr., was born on December 31, 1908, in New Haven, Connecticut, a month and two days after his father had accepted a call to become the seventeenth minister of the Abyssinian Baptist Church in New York. When Adam, Jr., was six months old, his family moved to New York, where he grew up and attended Townsend Harris Preparatory School before entering City College of New York at the age of sixteen. Because he overly involved himself in extracurricular activities, parties, drinking, and "being spoiled by women in new ways,"[1] his first and second semesters at City College were academic disasters. At that time he became quite disillusioned with school, and during

55

this critical period his sister, Blanche, whom he loved greatly, died.

Blanche's death was a tremendous shock to Powell. It turned him against everything and everyone, without reason or logic. He developed a hatred and mistrust of existence. At that point, he perceived the Bible as a jungle of lies and God as a myth. It seemed to him that the church was a fraud, and that his father was the leading perpetrator. He viewed his mother as a stupid rubber stamp and the smiling good people of the church as grinning fools. As a result of this inner turmoil, he withdrew from City College. Although this caused his parents great anxiety and disappointment, they refused to reject him. They became, instead, even more supportive, encouraging, and understanding. They agreed with Adam that what he needed was a change of environment and a chance for independence. With their support, he enrolled in Colgate University, where he became an honor student and graduated with distinction.

In February of 1931, while attending Colgate, he received the call to the ministry. Around 2:00 A.M., in his room in Andrews Hall, he heard a voice, "Whom shall I send? Who will go for me?" There in that room, for the first time in Powell's life, God talked to him. Powell said, "That day I began my first steps into areas of mysticism. And ever since, in every way, I've tried to maintain a sensitivity and an awareness so that this voice would always be heard."[2]

Powell did not stop his academic studies with the undergraduate degree but later enrolled in Teacher's College of Columbia University and received a master's degree in religious education.

Theology

Doctrine of the Church

One of the crises of the church historically has been the tension between maintaining the eternal truths of the

Christian faith and relating them to the social, political, economic, and educational conditions of society. The church should not become so progressive that it totally dissolves these eternal truths into society; on the other hand, it should not be so concerned with protecting these truths that it removes them from involvement in society. The proper approach is to maintain them and to relate them continually to the ongoing changes in society. This theological orientation combines spirituality with social phenomena and was operative in Powell's conception of the church. He defined his ministry in terms of the outreach of the church, which he said is at its best in "not just a Sunday-go-meeting church but a seven-day, twenty-four-hour-a-day church."[3] With this understanding, Powell felt that the church should be the microcosm of society, and its mission should be to make every attempt to actualize the eternal truths of God within society. He embraced a wholistic conception of the church and was critical of any attempt to separate spirituality from social reality.

Based on this concept, Powell led the members of his church toward a continual witnessing in all aspects of life, at all levels, with all people, in all places. In spite of its vast size, diverse history, and location in an unfriendly ghetto, the Abyssinian Baptist Church represented both a reservoir and a creative force of love and friendship throughout Harlem. "The outreach of our church is the outreach of a heart, as we move into the areas of our secular life—the mill, the factory, the office, the school, the bar, the club, the dance, politics; it does not matter where, we take this spirit with us."[4]

Powell was very critical of white churches that refused to involve themselves in the fight for social justice, and because of this refusal, he viewed the white church as one of the most hypocritical institutions in America, saying that it did more to impede than to facilitate the work of justice in society. "But the reason the Negro is more mature in his religion than the white man is that because of the white man's oppression of him, the Negro has been forced to make the search for God an everyday, twenty-four-hour job."[5]

Salvation and Liberation

What must I do to be saved? Is salvation an exclusive existential encounter between the individual and God? Or is it an existential experience with social transformation? Powell was careful not to separate the two. Salvation begins with the individual's realization of his sinfulness. Powell contended "that no man is better than any other man, that every human being is a sinner, that we are constantly in the process of sinning, that we sin by omission, we sin by commission, and we sin by permission."[6] Salvation begins when the individual comes into the knowledge of his finitude and frailties, expressing to himself his tendency toward sin. After one comes into that awareness, he develops a sense of guilt. While Powell recognized the validity of psychiatry and appreciated its contributions, nevertheless he firmly believed that sin or guilt can be cured permanently only through the power of God. The individual does not merit salvation through the religious experience; it is an unmerited gift from God.

For Powell, the experience of salvation was not perceived as a static event removed from social reality. He viewed it as a dynamic ongoing experience interwoven with social reality. It included liberation of the mind, soul, and body, thus moving the individual from unauthenticity into authenticity. The authentic experience realizes itself first in human relationships and social structures within society. It requires the actualization of justice within political, economic, educational, and social institutions. Powell said "There is absolutely no Christianity of any type in any church where there is not active and equal participation at every level of Church life and every level of religious institutions by all the sons of God."[7]

ADAM CLAYTON POWELL, JR. (1908–1972)

God and Eschatology

Powell argued that an awareness of God is essential for salvation. The presence of God, however, is nearer than one's hands and feet, and closer than one's breathing. The fundamental question then, is not the whereabouts of God, presupposing he is not near, but whether one is aware of the presence of God that penetrates existence itself. What is God? Powell thought of God as the beauty, truth, love, and goodness of the world. When one becomes aware of these qualities, then one is opening to the awareness of God. According to Powell, these qualities are both absolute and relative; their absoluteness means they are eternal, abstract, and complete. Their relativity means they realize themselves partially within society and continually participate within the ongoingness of society itself. In their absolute essence, these qualities represent the norm and standards for existence.

When a person encounters the presence of God, the salvation experience, as Powell perceived it, sets justice against injustice, love against hate, and goodness against evil. The Christian, therefore, he felt, should protest against all social, political, economic, and educational malfunctions that stand in opposition to the divine awareness.

The thrust of Powell's eschatology was of an earthly, or this-worldly, nature. He argued, "There is no heaven or hell in the sense that they are places to which one goes after death." His eschatology was geared toward the realization of God's possibilities for mankind within existence itself. He felt that if mankind would respond positively to the penetration of God, love, goodness, and social justice would become actualities. He embraced a realized eschatological vision, not looking for the triumphant eventuation of the kingdom of God beyond history, but contending that it was man's duty and responsibility to existentialize eschatology. His goal was the building of the "Great Black Society."[8]

Powell felt that the creation of a conscious level of black identity was essential to the development of that society; in this regard, he accepted the slogan of "black power." He thought of black power as an elevation of the consciousness of blacks to realize their dignity, pride, and self-respect. Following are fifteen of the essentials he perceived as being basic to the building of the Great Black Society, and which were the culmination of his eschatological vision for blacks on earth:

1. Blacks must develop the potential to lead their organizations, thus enabling the black community to control its own destiny and direction.

2. The black community must finance its own organizations.

2. Blacks must accept nothing less than the percentage of elected officials, jobs, and appointments equal to their proportion of the population.

4. Black people must support their own political candidates.

5. Black leaders in the North and South must work within the focus of the black revolution, through economic independence and political power. Adam used himself as an example of the kind of political power blacks should possess. As Chairman of the House Committee on Education and Labor, he controlled all labor legislation, including the minimum wage, and all education legislation: aid to elementary schools and higher education, manpower training and redevelopment programs, and vocational rehabilitation.

6. Blacks must become producers, in addition to being consumers.

7. Blacks should not accept outside leadership. Within their local communities, blacks should strengthen their leadership potential.

8. Black people should elect and follow only those leaders who are capable of sitting at the bargaining table, to

negotiate as equals for the black community's share of the loaf of bread, instead of begging for its crumbs.

9. Black leaders, including ministers, politicians, businessmen, doctors, and lawyers, must return to the black community; black communities all over the nation suffer greatly from "absentee black leadership."

10. Blacks must reject those ceremonial Negro leaders chosen by the white community.

11. In the fight to maintain a desegregated society, blacks must return to pride and participation in their own institutions.

12. All protest activity must be nonviolent.

13. No black person of voting age should be permitted to participate in a civil rights demonstration unless he or she is a registered voter.

14. Black people must oppose any laws of man that conflict with the laws of God.

15. Blacks must turn themselves toward development of their homes, churches, families, businesses, colleges, and neighborhoods.[9]

Political Career

On September 25, 1941, Powell announced his candidacy for the city council in the city of New York. Although registered as a Democrat, he ran as an independent candidate. When the returns of the election came in the first day, the *New York World-Telegram* ran a front page headline, "Powell Leads City." When the first ballot was counted, Powell came in third of ninety-nine candidates. His election marked the beginning of his distinguished political career.

Powell's next political step followed the redrawing in 1943 of the New York state congressional district boundaries. Previously, Harlem had been split into three districts and could not elect a black congressman. When the boundaries were redrawn, the Sixteenth Congressional District emerged, with Powell, the only black on the city council, as its natural candidate.

Elected without opposition in 1944, Powell went to Washington in January, 1945, as congressman from New York. He was reelected to Congress every two years after 1944, by margins as high as four-to-one, and never less than two-to-one.[10] In January, 1961, he became chairman of the House Committee on Education and Labor.

After twenty-three years of unbeatable and unsurpassed political strength, several serious charges were brought against Powell, and the House of Representatives authorized the Speaker of the House to appoint a special committee to investigate the allegations. The committee studied the situation carefully and arrived at the following conclusions:

First, Powell possessed the requisite qualifications of age, citizenship, and inhabitancy for membership in the House of Representatives and held a certificate of election from the state of New York.

Second, Powell had repeatedly ignored the process and authority of the courts in the state of New York in legal proceedings wherein he was a party, and his contumacious conduct toward the court on several occasions caused him to be adjudicated in contempt, thereby reflecting discredit upon, and bringing into disrepute, the United States House of Representatives.

Third, as a member of the House, Powell had improperly maintained Y. Marjorie Flores as clerk on his payroll from August 4, 1964, to December 31, 1966. During that period, she performed no official duties as required by law, in Washington or in the state of New York.

Fourth, as chairman of the Committee on Education and Labor, Powell had executed improper expenditures of government funds for private purposes.

Fifth, Powell's refusal to cooperate with the Select Committee and the Special Subcommittee on Contracts of the House Administration Committee in their investigation was considered conduct unworthy of a member.

Until the investigation was completed, Powell was refused the oath of office and was not permitted to take his seat in the House.

Upon its completion, the Select Committee made the following recommendations to the House:

First, that the Speaker administer the oath of office to Powell.

Second, that upon taking the oath of office as a member of the Ninetieth Congress, Powell be brought to the bar of the House to be publicly censured by the Speaker, in the name of the House.

Third, as punishment, Powell was ordered to pay the House $40,000; the Sergeant at Arms of the House was directed to deduct $1,000 per month from the salary of Powell until the sum of $40,000 was fully paid. These funds offset any civil liability of Powell to the United States government.

Fourth, the seniority of Powell in the House of Representatives was to commence as of the date he took the oath as a member of the Ninetieth Congress.

Fifth, if Powell did not present himself to take the oath of office on or before March 13, 1967, his seat was to be named vacant and the Speaker was to notify the governor of New York of the existing vacancy.[11]

Contribution

The contributions of Adam Clayton Powell, Jr., expanded into many areas of life. His long and distinguished career as a religious leader, politician, and servant of mankind has served as a milestone of hope for millions of Americans of various ethnic backgrounds. Powell was driven toward social justice, political awareness, and sensitivity for the poor, disadvantaged, and dispossessed

63

by parental influence and the social conditions of his day. He succeeded his father as pastor of the Abyssinian Baptist Church in New York City. In this capacity as minister to more than ten thousand people, he emerged as a significant spokesman in Harlem by the time he was twenty-three.

One night there was a knock on his apartment door, and he faced five prominent physicians, requesting community support because they had been banned from Harlem Hospital. The hospital served the black community with an all-white staff; these physicians were banned because they were black. Powell immediately organized the black community of Harlem around this incident. Community pressure and support resulted in an investigation, and the Board of Estimate eventually reinstated all five physicians, creating an interracial staff with a Negro as the medical director.

During the Great Depression, people were evicted by the thousands in Harlem. On the average, 150 people a day stood in line with eviction notices at Powell's office, and morning after morning, the curbstones of Harlem were lined with furniture of evicted tenants. Powell organized the Coordinating Committee for Employment to attack the problems of unemployment and discrimination. He led picket lines with the slogan Don't Buy Where You Can't Work! Membership in the Coordinating Committee for Employment immediately increased to at least 170,000 people. The efforts of this committee brought discriminatory hiring practices to a halt, and jobs were made available for blacks in restaurants, department stores, telephone corporations, public transportation systems, and many other areas.

When Powell was elected to Congress in 1944, he pledged to the people that he would push for racial equality, make every effort to eliminate restrictive covenants and discrimination in housing, attempt to establish a National Fair Employment Practices Commission and eradicate the poll tax, try to make lynching a federal crime, eliminate segregated transportation, make the thirteenth, fourteenth, and fifteenth amendments to the Constitution effective, fight every aspect of imperialism and colonialism, and protest the defamation of Protestants, Catholics, and Jews.

The greatness of Powell's political and religious careers rests in the fact that he was the people's man; he identified with the masses and dedicated himself to their service. He spoke to more than four thousand people when he preached at the Abyssinian Baptist Church. Because he brought a theological orientation to the masses, which involved the church significantly in the political, social, economic, and educational dimensions of society, the people supported him as their leader. Because of this support, Powell was in Congress for more than twenty years.

Part II
The Nation of Islam vs.
Black Christian Nationalism

Chapter VI
Elijah Muhammad (1897–1975)
Messenger of Allah

The success of The Honorable Elijah Muhammad as Messenger of Allah, and for many years the leader of the Nation of Islam, is one of the most unusual phenomena in the history of black America. During his lifetime he captured the attention of millions of both blacks and whites, nationally and internationally; few black Americans have been as powerful and as influential as Elijah Muhammad. What accounted for his success as a leader? What did he do that enabled him to become recognized immediately by many as the beginning and end of black leadership in America?

The book that best provides academic credibility for Elijah Muhammad's movement is C. Eric Lincoln's *The Black Muslims in America*, published in 1963. It immediately became the authoritative source on the Black Muslim movement, and is what Gordon W. Allport correctly describes as "one of the best technical case studies in the whole literature of social science."[1]

What were the social and historical factors that gave rise to the Black Muslim movement in America? In his study, Lincoln reported that in Detroit, there appeared a mysterious mullah, who referred to himself as W. Farad Muhammad. He told blacks in Detroit he had come from the holy city of Mecca, with a mission to teach blacks the truth about whites. He instructed blacks to prepare for the battle of Armageddon, which he interpreted to mean the final confrontation between blacks and whites.

The fame of Farad Muhammad spread rapidly throughout Detroit, and he established the first Temple of Islam during the Great Depression of the 1930s, when blacks were vulnerable to any philosophy that provided hope. Farad Muhammad, Lincoln pointed out, was perceived as the messiah or savior who had come to lead blacks into the millennium that is supposed to follow the battle of Armageddon. Very soon, however, Farad Muhammad had disappeared, and in his place came Elijah Muhammad, the new messenger of the Black Muslim movement. The movement began to develop great momentum and spread throughout America into most major cities, and Elijah Muhammad emerged as the Messenger of Allah and leader of the Nation of Islam.

Early Life and Development

There was nothing in Elijah Muhammad's early childhood that suggested he would become the apex of a major religious movement in America. He was born the son of a rural Georgia minister in 1897, and learned only the rudiments of reading, writing, and arithmetic before it was necessary for him to work in the fields to help support his family. At that time, neither he nor his parents suspected that he would soon emerge from a sharecroppers' patch in Sandersville, Georgia, to become one of America's most prominent black leaders.[2]

Theology

God

Elijah Muhammad was critical of blacks' acceptance of the Christian notion of God as a mystery or spirit; he felt this was misleading to those he referred to as the so-called Negroes. He also felt the word Negro was a misrepresentative term, designed by the white man to separate blacks from their Asian and African brothers. Further, he argued that American Negroes were not Americans, but were stolen from the Asian and African continents by white slavemasters.

Believing that all Christian teachings about God as a spirit were false, Elijah Muhammad contended that to resolve all doubt and suspicion, God made himself known in the person of Master W. Farad Muhammad. He referred to Master Farad as "God in person" and said that Allah sent Farad to save the so-called American Negro." He thought of Farad Muhammad as the Son of Man, whom the world had been expecting for thousands of years, to save those that were lost.[3]

When Farad disappeared from Detroit on May 26, 1933, at the peak of his influence, Elijah Muhammad said that he had been ordered out of Detroit, persecuted, and jailed. "He, Mr. W. F. Muhammad, [God in person] chose to suffer 3½ years to show his love for his people, who have suffered over 300 years."[4] After being ordered out of Detroit, Farad Muhammad went to Chicago, where he was arrested and suffered persecution also. Each time Farad was arrested, Elijah said Farad sent for him so that he, Elijah, could be properly instructed in the price of truth for American Negroes.

Allah is the name for God in the religion of Islam and in the teaching of Elijah Muhammad. Allah means "to submit," and the entire teachings of Elijah Muhammad were based upon complete submission to the will of Allah. "Nay, whoever submits his whole self to Allah and is a doer of good, he will get his reward with his Lord, on such shall be no fear, nor shall they grieve" (Holy Qur'an 2:112).[5]

Elijah Muhammad, the Messenger of Allah, taught his followers in the Nation of Islam, better known in America as the Black Muslims, that Allah is the one-hundredth attribute. He felt that Allah would make known to the world that he is God, and that beside him, there is no other. He also believed that Islam is the true religion of the world and that American Negroes would never be free until they recognized Allah as the true God, Islam as the true religion, and Elijah as the Messenger of Allah.

Man

Elijah Muhammad developed a doctrine of the person around an affirmation of blackness and a negation of whiteness. This approach was principally the result of Muhammad's belief that it was the black man's lack of knowledge about himself that kept him from enjoying freedom, justice, and equality. Believing it was Allah's will for the black man to know himself, Elijah Muhammad taught his followers that black Americans were descendants of the Asian black nation and of the tribe of Shabazz. The tribe of Shabazz, he contended, "came with the earth (or this part) 60 trillion years ago when a great explosion on our planet divided it into two parts. One we call earth and the other moon."[6]

Having grown up in Georgia when blacks were defined as "things" rather than as persons, and having experienced years of all forms of cruelty, discrimination, and hatred, Elijah Muhammad was very sensitive to the degree of inferiority impregnated upon the minds of black Americans. In order to lead blacks toward an escape from that feeling, he put most of his emphases on an appeal to blacks to love themselves and to accept themselves. Within this context, he developed programs in the Nation of Islam geared toward black history and other educational endeavors, economic development, and the need for black independence. In this regard, he developed a philosophy around the principle of "self-help."

Not only did Elijah Muhammad appeal to American Negroes to love themselves, but he also taught that "the original man, Allah has declared, is none other than the black man. The black man is the first and last, maker and owner of the universe."[7] Here, as is the case with other assertions, Elijah Muhammad doesn't employ any sociological, historical, or anthropological evidence to substantiate his claims. He merely makes the assertions and contends that "Allah has declared." The danger with this approach is that it creates a monologue, rather than a dialogue. It does not leave room for intellectual rigor and creative academic probing for truth. It is based on the premise that one does not question Allah; the individual simply submits and accepts Allah's truth, revealed through his messenger. Such a theology negates one of God's greatest gifts to humanity—the capacity to question, to disagree, to reject, or to accept.

Islam

Elijah Muhammad built the Nation of Islam around the religion of Islam. He perceived Islam as a religion of peace and truth. The word "Islam means entire submission to the will of Allah (God)." Elijah Muhammad claimed Noah, Abraham, Moses, Jesus, Job, David, Solomon, and Jonah as the prophets of Islam. He took the position that "the people of Islam are the black people, and their numbers are made up of the brown, yellow and red people, called races."[8] He felt that Islam meant salvation to each and every person who believed in it, and to the American Negro, he argued that Islam is the master key that opens all doors. He did not think of Islam as a religion alongside others; he thought of it rather as the one and true religion. He felt it would eventually dominate other religions and become the official true religion of the world.

Contribution

It is difficult to measure the contributions of Elijah Muhammad. His life's work is testimony to the magnitude of his involvement and influence on millions of black Americans. He has been included in this volume because of this significant impact.

In 1968, I was studying for the Master of Theology degree at the Boston University School of Theology. The black seminarians attending Harvard Divinity School, Andover Newton Theological School, Episcopal Theological School, and Boston University School of Theology hosted a consultation on the black church at Boston University that attracted black seminarians from throughout the country. One of the many speakers who addressed the consultation was minister Louis Farikan of Muhammad's Mosque No. 2, New York. We invited Farikan because not only did we as black seminarians want to understand the failures and successes of the black Christian community, but we also wanted to develop a more ecumenical spirit and a better working relationship with the Nation of Islam. After addressing the topic "Issues in the Muslim-Christian Dialogue," Farikan invited the black seminarians on a pilgrimage to Chicago to visit with Elijah Muhammad. McKinley Young, who was then a student at Andover Newton and serving as chairperson of the consultation, encouraged us to accept Farikan's invitation. Many of us were able to make the trip, and we looked forward with great anticipation to meeting Elijah Muhammad.

Upon arrival at his home, all of us were searched before we could enter. We were served a delicious meal, and then we began to talk about issues between black Christians and Black Muslims, only to discover immediately that from Elijah Muhammad's perspective, it was a monologue, not a discussion. We had good intentions and really wanted to establish a healthy ecumenical relationship between the two groups. Elijah Muhammad told us we could not work together as Muslims and Christians, because it was the will of Allah that all black Americans should be his followers. He said that Allah is the one true God and Islam the one true religion, and that

71

if we would accept Islam, we could work together. He declared himself the one true leader of black Americans and said that black leaders who were doing some good in society were only emulating his program.

After the meeting, I found myself disturbed over Muhammad's comments. In spite of my high regard and respect for him as a person and my great appreciation for his many contributions, I felt that his position was much too narrow, dogmatic, and insensitive to the many contributions of other black leaders. I had no intention of rejecting Christianity, and I certainly could not accept him as the one black leader. I perceived him as one significant black leader alongside others. He himself was influenced by Marcus Garvey, who preceded him.

But in spite of his closed mind and dogmatic philosophy, Elijah Muhammad made many lasting contributions. He developed a movement that has been recognized as one of the most organized and effective institutions among black Americans.

Elijah Muhammad died on February 25, 1975, and his son, Wallace D. Muhammad, became the new leader of the Nation of Islam. Wallace Muhammad not only has provided stability, vital direction, and leadership to the Nation of Islam, but he also has introduced innovative trends into its basic philosophy. One of them is the admission of whites. For years, Elijah Muhammad had taught that whites were devils and he was against any mixing of the races. To my knowledge he maintained this position until his death. Wallace is building on the great legacy of his father's contributions, but in addition, he is leading the Nation of Islam into new challenges which his father was not prepared to meet.

Chapter VII
Malcolm X (1925–1965)
Black Nationalist, Minister of Islam

Malcolm X is one of the best examples in American history of a self-made scholar, teacher, lecturer, and articulate spokesman for the freedom and liberation of blacks throughout the world. *The Autobiography of Malcolm X,* written with Alex Haley, author of the classic *Roots,* is a moving, penetrating, and disturbing narrative, for here Malcolm X exposed his most intimate experiences. It is difficult to understand and appreciate his beliefs fully, apart from an awareness of several significant events in his life.

Early Life and Development

Malcolm X was born on May 19, 1925, in Omaha, Nebraska. He was very devoted to his mother and had a high regard for the racial consciousness of his father. His father was a Baptist preacher and a follower of Marcus Garvey. His father "believed, as did Marcus Garvey, that freedom, independence and self-respect could never be achieved by the Negro in America, and that therefore the Negro should leave America to the white man and return to his African land of origin."[1] His continued outspokenness resulted in his sudden death shortly after the family moved from Omaha to Lansing, Michigan. Upon hearing that her husband had suffered fatal body and head wounds, Malcolm's mother became hysterical. Malcolm was only six years old at that time. His mother and the seven children suffered poverty, degradation, and oppression in the years that followed.

Malcolm attended public school in Lansing, where he was elected president of his class in the seventh grade and won popularity throughout the school as the smart "nigger boy." Even so, racism was part of his school experience. In relating an incident he said, "The one thing I didn't like about history class was that the teacher, Mr. Williams, was a great one for 'nigger' jokes. One day during my first week at school, I walked into the room and he started singing to the class, as a joke, ' 'Way down yonder in the cotton field, some folks say that a nigger won't steal.' " On another occasion, the class was studying a section on Negro history. Williams laughed throughout the entire section and referred to Negroes as ex-slaves, dumb, and shiftless. History was a favorite subject, but Malcolm lost all respect for his teacher.[2]

After completing the eighth grade, Malcolm left Lansing on a Greyhound bus for Boston. He later moved to Harlem, where he became involved in hustling of every form. He lived on the streets and found himself in a constant fight for survival; it was kill or be killed, take or be taken. He was involved in every racket—numbers, narcotics, robbery. In February, 1945, before he was twenty-one, Malcolm X was arrested for robbery and imprisoned for ten years. He was sent to Charlestown State Prison, and in 1948, he was transferred to Norfolk State Prison Colony in Virginia, which specialized in experimental rehabilitation. It was here that his brother, Reginald, introduced him to the Black Muslims and the teachings of Elijah Muhammad. His brothers and sisters had already accepted the teachings of Elijah Muhammad; they frequently visited Malcolm X at Norfolk and influenced him to write to Elijah Muhammad.

Malcolm X did write, and to his surprise, received a reply. Elijah Muhammad welcomed Malcolm X into the true knowledge, sent him $5.00, and told him that the black prisoner symbolized white society's crime of keeping blacks ignorant, oppressed, and deprived.

Malcolm X subsequently developed an unquenchable thirst for knowledge and understanding. He began by learning words from the dictionary and after completing the dictionary, he discovered that both reading and comprehension became easier. He attended classes at Norfolk State Prison, taught by professors from Harvard and Boston universities. Malcolm X determined to read every book in the prison library; he read day and night, with great obsession, such authors as Will Durant, H. G. Wells, W. E. B. DuBois, Carter G. Woodson, J. A. Rogers, Gregor Mendel, Frederick Olmstead, Herodotus, and Parkhurst. He studied Islam and the teachings of Elijah Muhammad with dedication. He said, "I had come to prison with 20/20 vision. But when I got sent back to Charlestown, I had read so much by the lights-out glow in my room at the Norfolk Prison Colony that I had astigmatism and the first pair of eyeglasses that I have worn ever since."[3]

After being released from prison, Malcolm X went to Detroit, to be near his family. He immediately began working to recruit members for the Detroit Temple No. 1 and received much recognition from Elijah Muhammad for his efforts. His original name, Malcolm Little, was changed by Elijah Muhammad to Malcolm X. The Muslim "X" symbolized Malcolm's true African name, which he never knew, and replaced the slavemaster's name, Little. Thereafter, in the Nation of Islam, the former Malcolm Little was known as Malcolm X.[4]

Malcolm X traveled quite frequently to Chicago to visit with Elijah Muhammad; they would talk for hours at the time. He studied diligently with Muhammad, not realizing that he was soon to become one of the most articulate and prominent spokesmen for the Nation of Islam. On countless occasions, Muhammad sent Malcolm X to represent him on television and radio programs and at public lectures. Because of his brilliant oratory, skill in debate, and militance, Malcolm X soon became an international figure in great demand. He appeared as guest lecturer on leading college and university campuses throughout the country, and also in public halls, forums, mosques, and churches.

Religious and Political Philosophy

In the first period of Malcolm X's religious and political philosophy, he was associated with the Nation of Islam as minister. During that time, he accepted and internalized the teachings of Elijah Muhammad. He said, "I have sat at our Messenger's feet, hearing the truth from his own mouth! I have pledged on my knees to Allah to tell the white man about his crimes and the black man the true teachings of our Honorable Elijah Muhammad. I don't care if it costs my life."[5] It was with this dedication and commitment to the teachings of Muhammad that Malcolm X launched his career.

Based on those teachings, Malcolm X contended that just as the evils of slavery had caused the destruction of ancient Egypt, Babylon, Greece, and Rome, so in this generation America's enslavement of twenty-two million blacks would bring her to her hour of judgment and her downfall as a respected nation. He felt it was God's divine will and power that destroyed the slave empires of ancient times, and that the same forces would also bring about the destruction of white America.

But before God could bring about this destruction, Malcolm X contended, the innocent must be separated from the guilty, the righteous from the wicked, the oppressed from the oppressor, and the slave from the slavemaster.[6] His entire religious and political philosophy at that point was based on this separatism. He argued basically for a polarization, or gulf between whites and blacks. Since he preached that the white world of supremacy was collapsing, he didn't think blacks could be saved from the wrath of God through white Christianity. In order for blacks to escape, he said, they must repent and accept Islam.

To accomplish this conversion, Malcolm taught that Allah was the one and only true God, and that The Honorable Elijah Muhammad was the only true messenger of Allah sent to save the lost sheep, meaning blacks, from the wrath of Allah. For this reason, he didn't compromise his position. He wanted blacks to repudiate Christianity and to accept both Islam and black nationalism as the only solution to the race problem in America. Here it is clear that Malcolm opposed any form of integration as a social, religious, or political philosophy. He accepted Elijah Muhammad's thesis that whites were devils and should not integrate with blacks. He opposed both the political and the religious systems of America. He had no faith in Democrats, Republicans, or independent parties, believing they all wanted to prey on blacks, and he called Allah to bring about the destruction of America.

Malcolm X vs. Elijah Muhammad

The religious and political philosophy of Malcolm X changed radically after his split with Elijah Muhammad. That split occurred when Malcolm X made a public statement about the assassination of President John F. Kennedy. After Kennedy's death, Elijah Muhammad had issued a directive to all Muslim ministers that they were not to make any remarks at all concerning the assassination. "Mr. Muhammad instructed that if pressed . . . , we should say: 'No comment.' "[7]

A national period of mourning followed the President's death. During that period, Elijah Muhammad was scheduled to speak in New York at the Manhattan Center. He canceled his appearance, but because the Nation of Islam could not be reimbursed for the rental of the center, he asked Malcolm X to speak in his place. The theme of his address was "God's Judgment of White America." During the question-and-answer period that followed, Malcolm X was asked his opinion of President Kennedy's assassination. Malcolm said it was a case of "the chickens coming home to roost."[8] He said that the hate in white men didn't stop with the killing of blacks but had struck down the nation's Chief of State. He insisted that the same hate had killed Medgar Evers and others. All over the nation, newspapers headlined "Black Muslims' Malcolm X: Chickens Come Home to Roost." Because of his disobedience, Elijah Muhammad silenced Malcolm X for ninety days. Malcolm accepted this discipline with humility, only to discover that Elijah Muhammad's plan was to silence him permanently.

Malcolm had been very disturbed over the disagreement with Elijah Muhammad. He and Muhammad were very close personally and had worked together through the years. Malcolm wanted to keep that relationship and to remain a member of the Nation of Islam. He acknowledged his mistake before Elijah Muhammad and repented, publicly expressed his regret at having made the statement, and expected, after the ninety-day suspension period, to become active again in the Nation of Islam. When he discovered that Muhammad had no intention of allowing him to return to business as usual, he called a news conference and announced his split with Elijah Muhammad and the Nation of Islam. He said, "I am going to organize and head a new mosque in New York City known as the Muslim Mosque, Inc."[9] The new organization, with temporary headquarters in the Hotel Theresa in Harlem, was geared toward the elimination of the political oppression, economic exploitation, and social degradation of black Americans.

MALCOLM X (1925–1965)

Malcolm's Pilgrimage to Mecca—
New Religious and Political Perspective

Every orthodox Muslim who can afford to do so is required to make a trip to Mecca at least once in his lifetime. In an effort to fulfill this obligation and to expand his religious understanding, Malcolm X decided to make the pilgrimage. His experience in Mecca changed his religious and political outlook. He observed that there were tens of thousands of pilgrims of all colors and races worshiping together, all participating in the same ritual, displaying a spirit of unity and brotherhood. The race problem was removed from the minds of the pilgrims by the religion of Islam. Malcolm said, "I have never before seen *sincere* and *true* brotherhood practiced by all colors together, irrespective of their color."[10]

What Malcolm X observed and experienced forced him to rethink much of his religious and political philosophy. While in Mecca, he ate from the same plate, drank from the same glass, slept in the same bed, and prayed to the same God as fellow Muslims, whose eyes were the bluest of blue, whose skin was the whitest of white, and whose hair was the blondest of blond. Malcolm concluded, "We were *truly* all the same (brothers)—because their belief in one God had removed the 'white' from their *minds,* the 'white' from their *behavior,* and the 'white' from their *attitude.*"[11] Malcolm X then thought that perhaps whites in America could accept the oneness of God and the oneness of man, and stop harming others because of their difference in color. He became convinced that America could profit from a true interpretation of Islam, because it erases the problem of race from society. "True Islam removes racism, because people of all colors and races who accept its religious principles and bow down to the one God, Allah, also automatically accept each other as brothers and sisters, regardless of differences in complexion."[12]

After the trip to Mecca, Malcolm X moved from a narrow,

79

exclusive religious and political orientation in the Nation of Islam to an open-minded inclusive approach. In the past, he had built his political thought around the principle of black nationalism and separatism. Now he began to think more about the political oppression, economic exploitation, and social degradation of blacks and others throughout the world. He sought to take the thrust toward freedom and liberation from a narrowly conceived black nationalistic mentality relegated to the United States and to make that thrust a worldwide concern, attempting to liberate all oppressed peoples. He argued that the issues of racism, oppression, and injustice should not be viewed merely as civil rights issues in America; rather, they should become human rights issues and should be brought before the United Nations for action. In visits to Egypt, Lebanon, Saudi Arabia, Nigeria, Ghana, Morocco, Algeria, and several other places, he had discovered that oppression was a worldwide problem, and not just a condition unique to the United States.

Malcolm X began his program by establishing the Organization for Afro-American Unity in New York on February 15, 1965, around the principle of freedom from oppression. All blacks were invited to become members, and urged to transcend whatever religious, political, or philosophical differences they might have and to unite around that principle. He did not require that one be a worshiper of Islam to join the organization. He then moved to an international effort to unify Africans and all oppressed people, based on the principle that oppression was a human problem and should be dealt with by the United Nations.[13]

Contribution

Within a very brief period, Malcolm X made an immeasurable impact on the world. Every segment of American society felt his influence. He was admired and respected by many, and hated and feared by others. He was, in fact, one of the most feared black leaders of this century. Along with the publication of *Black Muslims in America* by C. Eric Lincoln, Malcolm X brought both national and international recognition to the Nation of Islam. The controversy surrounding Malcolm X, along with his intellectual genius, greatly contributed to the popularity of the Nation of Islam.

Malcolm X was in great demand as a speaker and lecturer. Often he received more than twenty requests for speaking engagements in one mail. He traveled so much that his wife always kept a bag packed for him, so that when he returned from one round of speaking engagements, he could leave immediately for another. Throughout his tours, Malcolm always attracted large audiences, and the more controversial he became, the larger were his audiences. He argued and debated issues related to the Nation of Islam all across the country. While he served as one of its ministers, he was its foremost spokesman.

His painful split with Elijah Muhammad had a positive side, in that it enabled Malcolm X to articulate his own religious, social, economic, and political philosophy. He was then able to emerge as an intellectual giant in his own right. He was determined to continue to struggle for justice, freedom, and liberation of black Americans.

When Alex Haley was writing his life story, Malcolm X said he didn't think he would live to read it. He lived constantly under threat of death from both within and outside the black community. One might disagree with many of Malcolm X's ideas, but his courage, dedication, brilliance, and capacity to sustain himself in the midst of pressure demand respect and appreciation.

Chapter VIII
Albert B. Cleage, Jr. (1911–   )
Black Christian Nationalist

Elijah Muhammad influenced the lives and beliefs of many people. One of those is Albert Cleage, Jr., a United Church of Christ minister who is pastor of the Shrine of the Black Madonna in Detroit, Michigan. Although, as we will detect, many elements of his thought show Muhammad's influence, Cleage brought to the philosophy of black nationalism his own Christian understanding, with originality and creativity. Cleage sought to synthesize or to create a marriage between nationalism and Christianity. Was this possible without violating the basic principles of both? It was easier for Elijah Muhammad to synthesize black nationalism and Islam because of the problems that existed traditionally. Muhammad attacked Christianity on the basis that it was the white man's religion. As the convenient alternative, he projected Islam as the true religion for black Americans. Rather than abandoning Christianity, Cleage sought to make it more viable for black Americans by interpreting it from a black nationalistic perspective. It is from this perspective that Cleage should be viewed as a Christian nationalist.

Theology

Jesus

The publication in 1968 of Cleage's book, *The Black Messiah,* created much theological controversy within both black and white communities. Some dismissed it as sheer nonsense, some received it with mixed feelings, and others welcomed it. The controversial nature of the book centered around Cleage's interpretation of Jesus. He began by contending that for nearly five hundred years, Jesus was viewed from a white perspective, because the world was dominated by white Europeans. With the emergence of black nationalistic philosophies, Cleage argued that the truth about Jesus is finally revealed—"that Jesus was the non-white leader of a non-white people struggling for national liberation against the rule of a white nation, Rome."[1] He contended that the nation Israel was a mixture of Chaldeans, Egyptians, Midianites, Ethiopians, Kushites, Babylonians, and other peoples of color, and that these persons all were one with the black people of central Africa.

Who then was Jesus? Cleage interpreted Jesus to have been a black revolutionary leader, a Zealot who was seeking to lead a black nation to liberation and freedom. Looking toward the revitalization of the black church, Cleage maintained that the historic roots of the black church must be recaptured. He felt this would occur with the rediscovery of the black Messiah. He believed that with the black power movement in the 1960s, the black community was prepared to worship a black Jesus. "We could not follow a Black Messiah in the tasks of building a Black Nation until we had found the courage to look back beyond the slave block and the slave ship without shame."[2]

Elijah Muhammad built the Nation of Islam around repudiation of Christianity, the white slavemasters' religion, and the claim that Jesus was a prophet of Islam. Cleage, however, claimed Jesus to be a black revolutionary and defended Christianity. The rejection by many black Americans of Cleage's notion of the black Messiah added to the attractiveness of the Black Muslim movement. But Cleage pointed out that those black Americans who were race conscious enough to reject a white Christ "have been reluctant to embrace Islam in view of the role played by the Arabs in fostering and carrying on the slave trade in Africa."[3] It is apparent at this point that Cleage rejected Islam for reasons similar to those of Elijah Muhammad when he rejected Christianity. The two leaders, therefore, differed in religious philosophies, but did they differ in goals, purposes, and objectives? They were involved with similar tasks, in spite of their ideological differences.

In his efforts to interpret Jesus as the black Messiah, Cleage was attempting to help blacks to view Christ in their own image. He believed that only this kind of black Christian church would be capable of unifying the black community around liberation—that such a black church could influence each individual black person to unite with other black people to labor and sacrifice in the spirit of the black Messiah.

Nationhood

Cleage perceived his mission to be interwoven with that of the black church—to build a black nation. The black Christian church, he therefore argued, was the center of the black nation. This philosophy of black nationalism based on religious principles was fundamental to both Elijah Muhammad and Cleage. They simply approached it from different religious communities. The main point to grasp is that both were attempting to build a black nation. Cleage's program of nationhood was not nearly as effective as that of Elijah Muhammad, although Cleage did develop a large following of militant blacks and young radical college students.

He sought to build a black nation on the symbol of the black Madonna and Child, which would represent the future of the black nation. When a person joined the black church, Cleage said that individual was joining the black nation. He thought of the black church as a movement, or as the hub of the black nation, rather than as an institution.

For Cleage, the black church was significantly involved in a revolution toward nationhood. By revolution, he referred to raising the black consciousness from slave mentality to a new sense of selfhood, peoplehood, and nationhood. He argued that the black church must reinterpret its message in light of the black revolution. And, theologically speaking, Cleage believed that blacks must take the initiative toward building a nation, as opposed to waiting for God to intervene.

Unlike Elijah Muhammad, by nationhood, Cleage did not have in mind a physical or geographic location. For years Elijah Muhammad taught that Black Muslims should have a physical location within America. He wanted to build a black nation within a nation. But in later years, he seemed to have modified his position on the concept of black nationhood to connote any place where blacks existed. Cleage wanted to build something similar to a spiritual nation, with black Americans developing a sense of selfhood, loving and caring for one another, an identity, a feeling of being both spiritually and physically inextricably bound together.

Salvation as Corporate Experience

Critical of the apostle Paul, Cleage blamed him for much of the individualism found in Christianity. He viewed such individualism as the enemy of the philosophy of Christian nationalism. He also opposed Paul's spiritualization of Jesus and his preaching of individual salvation and life after death. It was Cleage's firm conviction that blacks, oppressed and degraded, do not need the individual salvation and otherworldly doctrines of Paul; they need instead to recapture the concept of nationhood found in the Old Testament, upon which Jesus built his teachings.

Continuing his strong repudiation of individualism, Cleage said that individuals cannot carry on revolutions; they can strike out at white society in episodic periods of frustration, but that is not revolution. Feeling that only a united people can carry on a revolution, Cleage contended that Black Christian Nationalism seeks to free the black community from the philosophy of individualism. He said, "The most important single aspect of both our faith and our program is the fact that we have rediscovered the process by which the individual can be led to divest himself of individualism and to merge into the mystic, communal oneness of the Black Nation."[4]

Cleage defined salvation as a corporate experience, as opposed to an individualistic experience. He called for blacks to confess the sin of individualism and to accept the corporate salvific experience of God at work within the black nation. For Cleage, to accept the salvific collective experience of nationhood was to accept a new birth of values inherent within the philosophy of Christian nationalism. He concluded, "A new Black church must call men from individualism to participation in a Black Liberation Struggle. The process by which we come to commitment is a part of our African heritage, including the method of Jesus and the Pentecostal group experience."[5]

Contribution

During the 1960s, when the black power movement was flourishing, Cleage made a significant impact on the black church. Having graduated from Wayne State University and Oberlin Graduate School of Theology, Cleage was intellectually prepared for the challenge to the black church presented by many young blacks and others. When Elijah Muhammad offered serious criticisms against the black church, arguing that the Christianity it practiced was not geared toward freedom and liberation for blacks, Cleage rose in its defense.

At one period during the 1960s, Stokely Carmichael emerged with great prominence and popularity as a civil rights worker and leader of black Americans. Stokely was a young black militant intellectual who marched with Martin Luther King, Jr., on many occasions and was at the time committed to nonviolence. But at some point he became disillusioned with both nonviolence and integration and called for black power as the most viable approach in achieving freedom and liberation for blacks. He traveled throughout the country advocating black power and developed a large following among black college students. Carmichael and his supporters were critical of Christianity and particularly of the black church. And here again, Cleage came to the defense.

Cleage said to Carmichael and to other black militants that the Christian religion they were rejecting was a slave Christianity that had no roots in the teachings of the black Messiah. He said to them that, based on his understanding of authentic revolutionary Christianity, they could be ordained in his church as civil rights workers if they could do away with the distinctions that existed in people's minds between what is religious and what is not religious. What would the ordination of civil rights workers mean? Cleage felt it would declare that the Christian church accepts their work as that of the church, and that those who give their lives in the struggle for human freedom are Christian. It would also mean, he said, that the civil rights movement is not only Christian but is part of the church, as well.

Part III
Black Religion, the Black Church, and Protest Ideology

Chapter IX
C. Eric Lincoln (1924–   )
Minister, Sociologist of Religion, Social Historian

E. Franklin Frazier, the noted sociologist who taught at Howard University for a number of years and produced more notably *The Negro Church in America*, *Black Bourgeoisie*, *The Negro Family*, and *The Negro in the United States*, died at the most critical period in the history of black Americans since reconstruction. Upon Frazier's death in 1959, black Americans were at the threshold of a new renaissance. A scholar with the dedication and intellectual rigor of E. Franklin Frazier was needed to interpret its social, historical, religious, psychological, and cultural dynamics. Gunnar Myrdal said it was most unfortunate that Frazier's premature death made it impossible for him to witness and comment on the rebellion of blacks against discrimination and poverty.

Scholars view C. Eric Lincoln as the successor to E. Franklin Frazier. As sociologist and historian, he has picked up where Frazier left off, providing an accurate analysis of black Americans in the 1960s, and continuing to do so today. Lincoln has given us a much needed interpretation of Martin Luther King, Jr., the Black Muslims, black power, and current trends in black religion. With his genius and intellectual rigor, Lincoln stands along with E. Franklin Frazier, W. E. B. DuBois, Carter G. Woodson, John Hope Franklin, and others.

Lincoln as Sociologist of
Religion and Social Historian

The Black Church vs. The Negro Church

E. Franklin Frazier's book, *The Negro Church in America,* still remains a valuable contribution to the study of Afro-American religious life. The book is a sociological study of the relation and role of religion in social organizations and structures among black Americans.

Lincoln, who is sincere in his role as sociologist of religion and social historian, does not agree with Frazier in his sociological methods and interpretations. Lincoln's book, *The Black Church Since Frazier,* published in 1974, grew out of the James Gray Lectures he delivered at Duke University in 1970. Frazier interpreted the Negro church, but Lincoln interprets the black church. What is the distinction? Are they mutually exclusive? Or are they in some way interrelated?

Lincoln argues that the Negro church Frazier interpreted does not exist today. "It died an agonized death in the harsh turmoil which tried the faith so rigorously in the decade of the 'Savage Sixties,' for there it had to confront under the most trying circumstances the possibility that 'Negro' and 'Christian' were irreconcilable categories." Lincoln contends that the sixties called black Americans to authentic personhood, thus forcing the Negro church to accept death in order to experience a rebirth. Does this mean then that the black church is merely the radicalization of the Negro church? On the contrary, Lincoln makes it clear that it is not. Rather, the black church is a critical departure from the norms of the Negro church. In spite of this departure, the Negro church that died in the moral and ethical holocaust of the 1960s "lives on in the Black church born of its loins, flesh of its flesh, for there are no disjunctions in religion."[1]

The word "Negro" depicts those norms, values, and life-styles imposed upon the black community historically and accepted by the black community as normative. The word "black" depicts a rejection of those imposed norms and a move toward self-identity, self-determination, self-respect, and the freedom to adopt new and authentic values emerging from the black community itself. The phrase "Negro church," as used by Frazier, represents one set of norms; the phrase "black church," as used by Lincoln, represents another set. At some points they appear to be mutually exclusive; sometimes they are in tension; and in other instances they appear to be interdependent and interrelated.

The Savage Sixties hit the Negro church with an urgent call to become sensitive to the crunch of nightsticks, the attacks by dogs, the barring of blacks from white churches, and the escalation of murder of blacks. Second, the call was for the Negro church to become disillusioned with a false sense of morality, to involve itself in the lives of black Americans, and to consign itself to its own identity and history. Thus, in the midst of the struggle of the sixties, the black church was born, in protest against discrimination, segregation, second-class citizenship, poverty, oppression, and unemployment.

Since its inception, the black church has been a diverse and complex entity, very similar to the diversity and complexity often found in the black community. A large element of the black church has always been conservative, passive, and uninvolved with the struggle toward black liberation. Another major segment has been involved significantly since its inception in the struggle of black Americans toward the achievement of freedom, justice, and equality. When Lincoln refers to the Negro church that Frazier interpreted, in large measure he is referring to the historically conservative, accommodative, and passive segment of the black church. The 1960s challenged the Negro church to die a shameful death and recapture its historic mission—to be the vanguard of social, political, and economic activism within the black community. In opposition to being uninvolved in the liberation struggle, the rebirth of the black church in the 1960s, as Lincoln clearly shows, made no disjunction between itself and the black community. It perceived itself as the spiritual and social force of that community. The significance of the black church does not lie in whether or not one is affiliated with it. Because of its centrality, the black church was historically, and continues today to be, the most potent force in the black community toward the attainment of justice, freedom, and equality for blacks.

Toward a Sociology of Black Religion

Not only has Lincoln continually provided scholarly assessments of diverse historic and contemporary phenomena related to black Americans, but he always has been on the cutting edge in interpreting and uncovering unexplored aspects of black religious thought. His monumental work, *Black Muslims in America*, brought before the world in a scholarly fashion the significance of a major religious sect that heretofore had not been recognized. W. E. B. DuBois pioneered in the area of sociology before it became a respected discipline. Lincoln, in his quest for a sociology of black religion, is pioneering in an unexplored area of black religious thought that has vast implications for the study of religion in America in general and black religion in particular.

Lincoln's effort in this regard is to examine certain important religious beliefs and practices of blacks in America against the background of functional theory. At the present time, Lincoln is working toward a prolegomenon to a functional theory of a possible sociological phenomenon, black religion. Before he can raise the question of the possibility of a sociology of black religion, Lincoln is quite aware of the need to establish the existence of black religion as a distinctive phenomenon. He says, "Now, it is a reasonable assumption that if black religion exists as a discrete religious phenomenon, then a sociology of black religion is possible, and if pursued ought to reveal something significant about the social implications of the religious understanding of Blackamericans."[2]

In establishing a viable sociology of black religion, Lincoln argues that it is necessary to substantiate the distinctiveness of such beliefs and practices among black Americans as their worship, myths, theodicy, God, cosmology, philosophy of history, and others. In this regard, it is inconceivable to many white Americans that blacks may possess a distinctive religion based on a corporate experience and a world-view different from traditional Protestantism. It is widely accepted that black religion is different and unique, but not that it is distinctive. This is a new approach to black religion. In fact, the idea that black religion possesses a distinctiveness about it is troublesome even to many blacks. On the other hand, there is a growing and increasing contention among black college students, black religious scholars, and black laypersons that the beliefs and practices of blacks are "authentically black—rejecting most black middle-class religious expression as white religion in blackface."[3]

One of the distinctive features of black religion is sharing. Of course, other religions participate in forms of sharing, but in the black church sharing is more intensified because of need, history, and tradition. This phenomenon in the black church is similar to that of religion itself among blacks. Religion is so dominant and potent that it is in order to say that blacks are fundamentally religious. To the same extent, sharing within the black church is just as basic.

Another distinctive aspect of black religion is its view of God. Black people adhere to a personal God who is a fighter and deliverer. This means "that black religion presupposes a God, who if He is not black in the sense of physical identification with this particular religious community, He is at least black-oriented in the sense that He is aware of their condition and assumes the leadership in setting things right."[4]

Ethnicity as practiced among black Americans takes

upon itself a distinctive quality. Religion in other cultures has promoted ethnicity; in the black community, it is the celebration of black culture and the black experience. It functions also, Lincoln continues, as the appreciation of blacks for who and what they are; it recognizes value within the black community itself, rather than risking psychological derailment by attempting to gain approval from the larger community. Black ethnicity finds value in the black experience that has been belittled and devalued by the larger community. An example of such unique experience is black worship.

Lincoln points out that most black church people desire a rousing sermon, along with moving song and fervent prayer, as essential parts of their worship service. During the service, many blacks want to feel free to let the Spirit enter their bodies and souls with thanksgiving. Because of this they find the conventional white worship services cold and uninspiring. For this reason, Lincoln feels that black ethnicity rejects white styles of worship and sanctions the ritual patterns that have been developed in black churches and that are independent of white church influence.

Religion in America

What are the historic roots of black and white religion in America? What are some of the factors within American history that contributed to the distinctiveness of black religion and white religion? Lincoln points out that any serious attempt to interpret and comprehend the religious situation in America must begin with at least the following two basic presuppositions:

(1) that Catholics, Protestants and Jews constitute the reigning religious triumvirate in America, and so perceive themselves; and

(2) that while all three groups have black constituencies of varying degrees of significance, the collective significance of blacks as Catholics, Protestants and Jews is seldom considered a meaningful factor in assessing the configuration of the religious mainstream in America.[5]

93

One of the points Lincoln is making here is that American religion has always been self-conscious of its racial exclusiveness and that it has traditionally disassociated itself from the religious proclivities of black Americans, even when various religious groups have been willing to accept the black physical presence in the worship service. Where then does black religion derive its relevance? Lincoln feels it comes from the inability to be included and accepted into the religious mainstream of America.

When did blacks become separated from the religious mainstream? Lincoln believes that they have always been excluded from it. "Two hundred years ago, despite the moving rhetoric of the revolutionary impulse, and despite the fact that thousands of black patriots fought and died for the cause, the American commonwealth, conceived in liberty for some, was born in slavery for others."[6] In light of this, America was conceived in the midst of contradictions. On the one hand, she was asserting, against the tyranny of Great Britain, that all are created equal, with certain inalienable rights. And on the other hand, she had stripped vast numbers of Africans of their humanity and political rights and was holding them in abject slavery. The separation of blacks from the religious mainstream in America started in slavery and continues even today.

During slavery, blacks were taught that it was God's will for them to be slaves. They were encouraged to accept Christianity only when it might make them docile, passive, and nonrevolutionary. After many blacks used Christianity as a force toward insurrection, it was made unlawful for slaves to worship without the presence of a white person. To avoid future revolutionary activity, blacks were allowed to attend white churches on a segregated basis. In those churches, blacks were consigned to galleries called "Nigger heavens" or to areas around the walls of the sanctuaries. They were not permitted to take communion with whites. Communion in this context means "the level of togetherness in which the individual self is transcended, merging with other selves in a common interest so profound and so meaningful as to blot out all distinctions of race, class, and personal circumstances."[7]

It was this constant separation that gave rise to the establishment of separate religions for blacks and whites, both under the heading of Christianity. In fact, the black church was born in protest against overt racism and discrimination within the white church. In 1787, Richard Allen, the founder of the African Methodist Episcopal Church, and Absalom Jones walked out of St. George Methodist Episcopal Church in Philadelphia, taking a group of blacks with them, because they had been degraded and segregated. In 1796, James Varick and Peter Williams withdrew from John Street Methodist Church in New York City and organized the African Methodist Episcopal Zion church, because they had been refused communion with whites at the chancel rail.

Contribution

C. Eric Lincoln is unusually involved in scholarly, civic, social, ministerial, civil rights, and professional activities. In terms of intellectual stature, broad influence, and impact, Lincoln stands as one of the foremost sociologists of religion in this country. He is one of the most sought-after scholars in his field, and he finds himself in more demand than he can humanly accommodate. Based on his publications and influence, Lincoln has lectured at more than one hundred of the leading institutions of higher learning throughout the world. Additionally, he has appeared as guest lecturer for professional societies and organizations across the country. He is one of the few blacks to be elected a Fellow of the distinguished American Academy of Arts and Sciences. One of his many other achievements is his election to Who's Who in the World.

Lincoln's educational background includes LeMoyne College, Fisk University, The University of Chicago, and Boston University, where he earned the Ph.D. degree in sociology of religion and social ethics. His dissertation, *The Black Muslims in America*, was published and marked the beginning of his distinguished career. Additionally, he has written eight other major books, innumerable chapters in volumes for symposia, and many scholarly articles in major professional journals and magazines.

He originated and serves as editor of the C. Eric Lincoln series in black religion, which has led to the publication of seven major volumes on various aspects of the subject: Harry V. Richardson, *Dark Salvation*; William R. Jones, *Is God a White Racist?*; Leonard E. Barrett, *Soul-Force*; Gayraud Wilmore, *Black Religion and Black Radicalism*; Joseph R. Washington, *Black Sects and Cults*; Henry H. Mitchell, *Black Preaching*; and James H. Cone, *A Black Theology of Liberation*.

Chapter X
Charles Shelby Rooks (1924–   )
Minister, Educator,
Seminary President

A crisis facing the black church since its inception has been the lack of theologically trained leadership. The majority of black clergy serving black churches do not have a theological education. Although within recent years the percentage of trained clergy has radically improved, this trend has not had a significant impact on the masses of black churches. There are many factors contributing to this problem. Charles Shelby Rooks has pioneered in dealing with the complexity of the black church and theological education.

Early Life and Development

Born in October, 1924, at Beaufort, North Carolina, the son of a Presbyterian minister, Charles Shelby Rooks' formative years were spent in Christian nurture. He was educated at Virginia State College, Petersburg, Virginia, and Union Theological Seminary in New York City. He has done additional study at Teachers College, Columbia University, and at Mansfield College, Oxford University, England.

Ordained to the Christian ministry in the United Church of Christ in September, 1953, Rooks began his career by serving as pastor of the Shanks Village Protestant Church in Orangeburg, New York. He later served as pastor of Lincoln Memorial Congregational Temple, Washington, D.C. The impact of Shelby Rooks upon black clergy and theological education began with his appointment as associate director of the Fund for Theological Education. He was appointed executive director in 1967 and served in that capacity until his appointment as president of Chicago Theological Seminary in 1974.

Religious Philosophy

The Black Church and the Black Preacher

The black church is one of the oldest and most influential institutions within the black community. The black church was born in protest against discrimination and other oppressive forces, and played a vigorous and determinative role in the quest for freedom of blacks in America. Shelby Rooks argues that the black church continues to be a major factor on the contemporary scene, and that it will inevitably be involved significantly in developing the new and emerging direction of blacks.[1] Basic to the great legacy and importance of the black church in social change, the black preacher historically has been perceived by the black community principally as a social-change agent.

It is Rooks' contention that "the black minister is expected by the black church and the black community to provide leadership, energy, and wisdom in the struggle to change the oppressive economic, social, and political burdens of black life in America."[2] The goals and expectations of the black preacher as change agent have been historically a part of what Rooks calls "intuitive ecclesiology," rather than an articulated one. This means that although black preachers historically have assumed the role, they have not examined it critically. In the past, because of the nature of blacks in America, intuitive

98

ecclesiology was probably sufficient, but conditions have changed.

Rooks makes it emphatically clear that during slavery, the black church had to build a strong black community with sufficient resistance to counteract the effects of dehumanization and to provide a means of survival. The black church developed the community's social and religious dimensions, as well as provided encouragement and hope for freedom. In the slave community, the black church was more than a voluntary institution—it was the only agent for rationality and survival.

Rooks shows that the basic function of the black church remained essentially the same throughout the period of reconstruction. Since that era brought no essential relief from the shackles of slavery to the black community, the church had to continue to provide hope for personal survival, religious and social development, and activity toward freedom. The intuitive ecclesiology of the black church also remained the same.

The break in this pattern occurred in the twentieth century with the elimination of legal segregation and discrimination in education, employment, and public accommodations. However, even now, the fundamental problems of oppression continue, though in a different form. The old symbols have collapsed, which requires the black church to rethink its ecclesiology. The problem before it now is the pressing need to define and clarify what it means for blacks to exist in America today, in the face of subtle oppression. In light of this, what direction politically, socially, educationally, and economically should the black community take? What guidance can the black church provide? Should the black community move toward integration? Should it move toward separation and nationalism? Or should it become indifferent about its direction?

Rooks feels that the doctrine of the black church for the contemporary situation in America must be focused around new life for blacks. "The structure, doctrines, and liturgy of the black church must be constructed, then, to create new life for black people in this social context, and the essence of that context is economic, social and political."[3] He challenges black clergy and laity alike to confront the indirect forms of oppression. The task of the church, therefore, is to clarify, by articulating its ecclesiology, the new emerging role of the black preacher as change agent.

What is the contemporary black preacher attempting to change? The goal of the black church has always been geared toward freedom and liberation. Presently, Rooks says correctly that the content of that freedom needs clarification. At one point in the history of black America, freedom meant simply liberation from the chains of slavery. In another period, it meant liberation from legal segregation and discrimination. What does the black church mean by "freedom" today? At this point, Rooks pushes the black church to define its goal and develop viable ways of achieving it.

Rooks continues his challenge with the contention that the achievement of the goals and expectations of the black church require cooperative rather than individualistic models of ministry. He argues that the individualistic style of leadership embraced by the black preacher historically has been both a great strength and a weakness in the church. "Without charismatic, and usually religiously charismatic, leadership we might still be in chains. The freedom of the black church has enabled individual leaders to emerge and to provide us with imagination, hope, and the example of great courage."[4] Yet, the very historic examples themselves, Rooks feels, attest to the fact that individualistic styles of black leadership have proved disastrous to the development of continuity and consistency.

That style of leadership, according to Rooks, has within it the seeds of self-destruction. The model is inherently exclusive, egotistic, and triumphal. It demands confidence in the leader that his goals are correct, his style is right, and that his method is the only way to accomplish the goal. Every competitive leader is seen as either less correct or incorrect. "Consultation or conference may occur, as in the case of the staff of the Southern Christian Leadership Conference, but neither the organization nor the effort can progress if there is fundamental disagreement with the basic goals and philosophy of the individualistic leader."[5] Rooks says that if anything happens to an individualistic leader, the organization dies or becomes ineffective. The possibility of immediately finding a replacement is unlikely, because that style of leadership does not systematically cultivate leaders.

Another weakness of the individualistic style is that the leader can be destroyed easily by determined persons. America has used every tactic to destroy strong, charismatic, vibrant, outspoken, black individualistically oriented leaders. One tactic has been the subversion by offers of power and money. Another tactic has been murder, such as that of Martin Luther King, Jr. Others have been vilification, harrassment, and frustration. On the contrary, Rooks proposes cooperative models of leadership. He feels that "cooperative leadership models involving the minister as a member of a change agent *team*, rather than as an individual, are absolutely required."[6]

Rooks' position is that the demands placed upon the black preacher as change agent are more complex today than they were in the past. The contemporary situation demands that the black preacher empower the laity to assume change roles. In order to maximize the resources of the black church, each member must participate significantly in the change-agent process. This will enable the black church to regain its historic sense of corporate wholeness. Since the black preacher cannot know everything, he needs to interface his role as change agent with experts in such fields as politics, business, government, education, economics, and community development.

101

Theological Education and the Black Church

A major problem facing the black church is a shortage of theologically trained clergy. The reason for this problem is very complex. Many blacks adhere to a mystical concept of "the call" and feel they don't need a theological education to preach the gospel. This group tends to think that God prepares them to preach, apart from any formal training. Many black denominations do not have a formal theological education as a requirement for ordination. The majority of black clergy serving black churches lack theological degrees, although black clergy serving black congregations in predominately white denominations, such as the United Methodist, American Baptist, Episcopal, Roman Catholic, Presbyterian, and others are required by those denominations to have theological degrees. But the black clergy in these denominations are in no way representative of the masses of black clergy.

Predominately white seminaries have not always admitted blacks. Some white seminaries have recently produced their first black graduates. Traditionally, the few blacks seeking theological training have attended one of the three major black seminaries: The Interdenominational Theological Center in Atlanta; Howard University School of Religion, Washington, D.C.; and Virginia Union University School of Religion. These are the only fully accredited black theological seminaries in the country. Others, such as Hood Theological Seminary and Shaw University School of Religion are associate members of the Association of Theological Schools. A great percentage of black graduates are produced annually by these seminaries.

The Interdenominational Theological Center was chartered in 1958 by four participating theological schools: Gammon Theological Seminary (United Methodist); Morehouse School of Religion (Baptist); Phillips School of Theology (Christian Methodist Episcopal); and Turner

Theological Seminary (African Methodist Episcopal). Since that time, three other seminaries have become affiliated with the Center. They are Johnson C. Smith Theological Seminary (United Presbyterian Church in the U.S.A.), Charles Harrison Mason Theological Seminary (Church of God in Christ), and Absalom Jones Theological Institute (Episcopal).

In September, 1960, Shelby Rooks left his church in Washington, D.C., to assume responsibility for recruiting black students for theological seminaries and for administering a national program of financial aid for their support, working under the auspices of the Fund for Theological Education. His position with the Fund grew out of a concern on the part of several key persons for the need to increase the enrollment of black students in theological seminaries. Attempting to deal systematically with this concern, financial support from the Lilly Endowment enabled the Department of Ministry of the National Council of Churches to bring seventy churchmen, black and white, together in a consultation in March, 1959, at Seabury House in Connecticut.

Rooks reports that from that consultation emerged a recruiting and fellowship program for blacks in theological education, underwritten by the Sealantic Fund, Inc., and administered by the Fund for Theological Education, under the auspices of the Rockefeller Foundation. The Sealantic Fund contributed to the financial support of "The Interdenominational Theological Center in Atlanta to the tune of several million dollars over a period of ten years, and the support of the fellowship activities of the Fund for Theological Education, specifically on behalf of blacks, in the amount of nearly two million dollars by the end [of 1974]."[7]

According to Rooks, by 1963 the Fund for Theological Education had supported 190 blacks who received fellowship awards in first professional degree programs, and thirty-five additional persons at the doctoral level.

These figures are much more significant to date. The Fund has continued its commitment and dedication to the support of blacks in theological education as one of its emphases. In light of this landmark, Rooks said, while serving as executive director, "I want publicly to pay tribute to it for both its quantity and consistency for it is virtually the only significant base of financial support blacks have had in theological education up to this point, and it has been profoundly important."[8]

Rooks made a concentrated effort to expand the enrollment of blacks in white seminaries, and was very successful in his efforts. Because of his untiring dedication and commitment, many white seminaries reexamined their admission and financial-aid policies to accommodate blacks, and made adjustments in their curriculum to include black studies. Had it not been for the financial support and encouragement provided by the Fund for Theological Education, many blacks would perhaps not have attained a seminary education. Although Rooks was very successful in persuading white seminaries to increase their enrollment of blacks, he did experience some serious difficulties.

Those experiences led him to question whether black men and women are ever to be prepared adequately for the Christian ministry in terms of the unique and distinct needs of the black community, and whether black students and professors should separate themselves from white theological schools and seek an environment where they can deal creatively with the problems of the black struggle. Writing in 1969, he said, "Nothing that has happened in American theological education leads me to believe that white seminaries will ever regard black Christianity as something central to their main interests, will ever seriously attempt to relate significantly to black Christians."[9] On what facts did he base this assertion?

In the first place, Rooks wanted to approach the problem from a skeptical perspective, in an attempt to bring to the surface the intensity and magnitude of the problem. He wanted white seminaries to realize that all their efforts toward recruitment and admission of blacks represented only an inadequate and overdue attempt to resolve a major problem. Second, at the height of his efforts in this direction, in 1969, he realized that not more than twenty or twenty-five black undergraduates were enrolled that year in any single white seminary. Of the three hundred black students enrolled in ninety-five fully accredited seminaries, at least half were enrolled in two black seminaries. The other half were scattered throughout the ninety-three other seminaries.

Third, only a dozen of the ninety-three seminaries mentioned had any black professors on their faculties; the production rate of black faculty members was extremely low. A survey completed in the summer of 1968 revealed "that in the period between 1953 and 1968 only 39 black Americans received the Ph.D. degree in religion at all the seminaries and graduate religion departments in the U.S. and Canada—an annual production rate of 2.60."[10] The 1977–78 Fact Book on Theological Education reports that in 1970 there were 808 blacks enrolled in theological seminaries and in 1977, 1,759 were enrolled, showing that the increase in black enrollment has been very modest. "Black students still number only 3.9% of that student body, far below their percentage in the population at large."[11] In light of the increasing number of black churches that become vacant each year all over the United States in each denomination that has the black presence, the number of blacks enrolled in theological seminaries is far too low to begin to accommodate the need.

In his effort to recruit blacks for theological seminaries, Rooks found himself with a dilemma. He wondered if the emphasis should be put on the separation of black seminary students and professors into all-black situations so that the particular needs facing the black church could be addressed more significantly; or should the emphasis be

105

on reforming white seminaries and equipping them to consider the black religious experience? Rooks determined to focus on attempting to reform white seminaries within an integrated context. He doubted the possibility of developing enough unity among black professors and students to make separation a significant alternative. He felt there was too much disagreement among blacks as to its dignity—"even if that separation is viewed as a temporary expedient."[12] Also, Rooks realized that most blacks, including himself, were not ready for the great sacrifices a separation would involve.

In order to persuade white seminaries to deal seriously with the black religious experience in an integrated context, Rooks suggested that four major areas needed improvement. First, there must be wider participation of blacks in the decision-making processes of theological education. Here he referred to the need for black representation on boards of trustees, faculties, and administrations of white theological schools. Second, we must find ways to increase significantly the number of blacks enrolled in both black and white seminaries. Third, curriculum in white seminaries must reflect not only a realization of the worth of the black church, but also a willingness to come to grips with a creative new style of life for the black church. Fourth, the placement of blacks upon graduation should be improved to enable the seminaries to better serve the church.

Contribution

It is very difficult to measure the great impact Charles Shelby Rooks had on theological education during his tenure as associate and executive director of the Fund for Theological Education. He pioneered in encouraging blacks to acquire a theological education before many white seminaries were admitting blacks. As executive director of the Fund, he had an opportunity to interview all black recipients of the Protestant Rockefeller Fellowship in Religion. This enabled him to assess the students' promise as ministers. When many white seminaries became aware of the tremendous support the Fund for Theological Education was providing for black students, they began to respond favorably to recruiting and admitting more blacks.

Another undertaking of the Fund was the Black Doctoral Program in Religion, launched as a result of the dedication and commitment of Rooks, under the auspices of the Rockefeller Fellowship Program. Its main purpose was to encourage seminaries and graduate schools in religion to admit qualified blacks to the doctoral program and to encourage potential black scholars in religion to consider the Ph.D. The main focus of the program was on scholarly research, teaching, and publication. Its graduates are now serving in teaching, administrative, and research capacities in theological schools, colleges, universities, and research centers throughout the United States.

It has been one of Rooks' convictions that the black church and black religion, with all their creativity and promise for the future of religion in America, need to be informed by the best of scholarly research, intellectual rigor, and theological reflection. With this conviction, he led black scholars toward the creation of the Society for the Study of Black Religion, a professional organization committed to the pursuit of scholarly research, and was its founder and first president.

After spending many devoted and dedicated years as executive director of the Fund for Theological Education, Rooks was invited to become president of the Chicago Theological Seminary. He accepted that appointment and presently influences theological education on a larger and broader level.

Part IV
Theology of Nonviolence and Direct Action

Chapter XI
Martin Luther King, Jr. (1929–1968)
Minister, Systematic Theologian,
Nobel Peace Prize Laureate

One of the statements that best captures the breadth of the life of Martin Luther King, Jr., was given at his funeral by his mentor and lifelong friend, Benjamin Elijah Mays. King and Mays had agreed that one would eulogize the other, depending on which of them lived longer. Mays said, "It isn't how long one lives, but how well. It's what one accomplishes for mankind that matters."[1] Martin Luther King, Jr., died at 39. During his brief lifetime, he stressed the belief that God has endowed all persons with possibilities that need to be developed, organized, and realized to their highest capacity. Each person has a contribution to make to the human race, and mankind cannot fulfill itself until everyone maximizes the actualization of those possibilities. It was this sense of commitment and dedication that enabled King to rise to the highest level in realizing the potential within himself.

Early Life and Development

King was an exceptional student in high school. He skipped the ninth grade at Booker T. Washington High School in Atlanta, passed a college entrance examination, and skipped the twelfth grade, completing his high school work at the age of fifteen. He then entered Morehouse College in Atlanta. At Morehouse, not only did King receive an excellent liberal arts education that served as the foundation for his graduate training in theology, but he was also exposed to noble ideas, lasting values, rigorous competition, and a philosophy of education geared toward humanization and the establishment of the dignity of the individual. It was at Morehouse College that King and Mays established their lifelong friendship. King greatly admired Mays and was fascinated with his wisdom and approach to life situations. Along with hundreds of other students, King frequently listened to Mays attentively in chapel services. Mays encouraged the students, challenged them, and instilled within them a feeling of pride, self-respect, and a compelling drive to succeed in life, regardless of the obstacles. As president of Morehouse, Mays firmly believed that not only should a college develop intellect, but it should build character as well. This philosophy of education penetrated Morehouse College and left a lasting impression on King; he was also greatly influenced by George D. Kelsey, who was then director of the department of religion.

When he began to consider a career, King did not give the ministry top priority; rather, he felt negatively about it. Although his father was the prominent pastor of Ebenezer Baptist Church in Atlanta, King rebelled at the idea of the ministry as a vocation. He was a sociology major and thought of becoming a lawyer. Deep within himself, however, King had the desire to be a minister, although "he was still repelled by the 'emotionalism,' the hand-clapping, 'amen-ing,' and shouting of the Negro Church. Moreover, he believed that there was an oversupply of 'unintellectual' and 'untrained ministers' in the Negro Church."[2] But both Mays and Kelsey were trained black ministers with social consciousness, and that inspired King to rethink the ministry as a possible vocation. Then

109

after meditation, contemplation, and experiencing the call to the ministry, King accepted it as his life's work.

After making that decision, King chose to study at what was then Crozer Theological Seminary in Chester, Pennsylvania. Crozer has now merged with Colgate Rochester Theological Seminary in Rochester, New York. At Crozer, he was an exceptional student, making straight As and graduating first in his class. He was the recipient of the Crozer scholarship and chose Boston University to study for the Ph.D. degree in systematic theology.

It is important to emphasize the fact that King was a trained systematic theologian. Many people think of him as a social ethicist because of his social activism. It is true that he was drawn more and more toward social ethics, but his formal training was in systematic theology. Having done his Ph.D. dissertation on "A Comparison of the Conceptions of God in the Thinking of Paul Tillich and Henry Nelson Wieman," King was equipped with a highly sophisticated theological orientation. After his death, several schools instituted Martin Luther King, Jr. professorships in several disciplines, but none of them were in the area of King's major. Boston University, his alma mater, founded a Martin Luther King, Jr. Professorship in Social Ethics. And Colgate Rochester Divinity School established a Martin Luther King, Jr. Professorship in Black Church Studies. Why weren't these professorships in King's formal discipline, systematic theology?

Traditionally, theological schools have associated social ethics and practical theology, rather than systematic theology, with social activism. King brought theology as a discipline from its traditional noninvolvement in the social conditions of humanity into the cutting edge of social reform. He brilliantly translated theory into practice. His theological presuppositions did not end in contemplation and abstraction, as those of many theologies tend to do; his theories took concrete form as they manifested themselves in the actual social, political, economic, and educational structures of society.

Influences on King's Theology

At Boston University, King studied principally under L. Harold DeWolf and Edgar S. Brightman. Both men influenced him greatly and stimulated him in the area of personalistic philosophy—"the theory that the clue to the meaning of ultimate reality is found in personality." King contended that personalism was his basic philosophy— namely, its "insistence that only personality—finite and infinite—is ultimately real."[3] This strengthened King in two convictions: it gave him metaphysical and philosophical bases for belief in a personal God, and it gave him a metaphysical basis for belief in the dignity and worth of all persons.

Brightman taught a course on the philosophy of Hegel each year, and just before Brightman's death, King took the course. Although both Brightman and King disagreed with many points in Hegel's thought, both were fascinated with his entire philosophical system. Absolute idealism repelled King, but he was much influenced by Hegel's dialectical methods, particularly the principle of "creative tension."

Any student of philosophy knows that Hegel's philosophical system is fundamentally politically conservative; it doesn't lend itself to revolutionary activity. This brought about the nineteenth-century breakdown of the Hegelian philosophical system that led to the development of left- and right-wing Hegelians. Karl Marx, a left-wing Hegelian, reversed the absolute idealism of Hegel into a thorough-going materialism. In other words, Marx turned Hegel's philosophical system upside down. Marx retained the creative tension principle in Hegel's dialectical method but replaced the mystical metaphysical idealism with economic and social reality. King was a student of both thoughts although he did not adopt either system exclusively.

King rejected Marx's materialistic interpretation of history. He opposed both Marx and the Communist repudiation of God. King argued, "As a Christian I believe that there is a creative personal power in this universe who is the ground and essence of all reality—a power that cannot be explained in materialistic terms." He believed, as a Christian and in keeping with Hegel's philosophy, that all history is ultimately guided by spirit, not matter. He opposed Communism's ethical relativism and contended that because there is no divine government in Communism and no absolute moral order, almost anything is a justifiable means to an end, whether it be violence, deception, or murder. King rejected the political totalitarianism of the Communist system, and argued, "True, the Marxist would argue that the state is an 'interim' reality which is to be eliminated when the classless society emerges; but the state is the end while it lasts, and man only a means to that end. And if any man's so-called rights or liberties stand in the way of that end, they are simply swept aside."[4]

In spite of the shortcomings of Marx's philosophy, it raised some basic questions for King that stayed with him throughout his life. It gave him a sharpened insight into the gulf between extreme wealth and abject poverty, and it also made him sensitive to the tendency in capitalism to be more concerned with making a living than with enriching a life.

Another aspect of Hegel's thought that influenced King was the notion of "creative synthesis." Regardless of the nature of the particular crisis he faced, King always looked for a creative synthesis—harmony, unity, and wholeness. While he confronted all forms of segregation through direct action and nonviolent protest from the antithesis, he looked for the synthesis within the political, social, economic, and educational structures of existence. Both the Hegelian and Marxist philosophical systems move toward a creative synthesis. It would not be proper, however, to designate King as either a Hegelian or a Marxist. As a scholar exposed to a multiplicity of philosophical and theological systems, he constantly employed several in his own creative and original manner. Although he rejected elements of Hegel and Marx, he appreciated some aspects of both systems.

King was also influenced by the theologian Reinhold Niebuhr, who was one of the exponents of the neoorthodox theology of the early twentieth century. King rejected Niebuhr's tendency to view human nature from the perspective of depravity, but he also rejected the liberal conception of human nature that was the antithesis of the neoorthodox view. King developed a synthesis of the two positions. L. Harold DeWolf, King's professor at Boston University, touches on this point when he says, "King rejected Niebuhr's 'Christian realism' which had the effect of compromising disastrously with the world's evil, and even of defending the nuclear arms race. Neither the thesis of liberal optimism nor of Neibuhrian 'realism' would do."[5] The basic philosophical position that King accepted was a synthesis of the personalistic philosophies at Boston University, especially those of L. Harold DeWolf, Edgar S. Brightman, Allan Knight Chalmers, and Walter G. Muelder.

A careful examination of King's dissertation on Tillich and Wieman shows his fundamental theological problems with both thinkers. However, he was influenced considerably by the thought of Henry David Thoreau and of James Russell Lowell, and was well versed in the views of Walter Rauschenbush, although he considered Rauschenbush too optimistic about social progress.

The life and thought of Mahatma Gandhi also affected King greatly. After hearing a sermon by Mordecai Johnson in Philadelphia on the life and teaching of Ghandi, he began an intensive study of Ghandi's belief and eventually conceptualized the possibility of applying the philosophy of nonviolence to the race problem in America. He believed Ghandi was the first person in history to lift the love ethic above mere interaction between individuals to become a force for social reform. Ghandi's philosophy of nonviolence became the focal point for King's approach to the subject.

Another very powerful influence on King's life and convictions was the black religious tradition from which he emerged. It is important to note that his fundamental desire, as his career began to take shape, was to pastor. He came from generations of preachers; he was the son, the grandson, and the great-grandson of preachers. Preaching and oratory came naturally to King. He was stimulated and motivated by the rich tradition of black religious leadership to which he was heir. His father greatly inspired him, both during his formative years and in later years. After the completion of the residency work for his doctorate, several colleges expressed an interest in King. He was offered a professorship, a deanship, and an administrative position, but he accepted a call to become pastor of Dexter Avenue Baptist Church in Montgomery, Alabama, because he wanted to pastor, and also because he was interested in returning to the South. It is correct to interpret King as a systematic theologian, an orator, a humanitarian, and a universalist, but equally important is the fact that he was a preacher and the product of the great legacy of black religious leadership.

King and the South

King had no intention of setting into motion events that would shake the foundations of the South, the nation, and the world. He wanted to be a good pastor, not a revolutionary, although he had always had a social consciousness and an interest in eliminating injustice, segregation, oppression, and racism. His father had instilled those ideas in his mind when he was very young.

What were the conditions in Montgomery and Birmingham when King returned? In Montgomery, King reported that of the approximately seventy thousand white people, the median income in the middle 1950s was $1,730, compared with $970 for the fifty thousand blacks. The black and white communities of Montgomery moved on separate paths. The public schools were still segregated in spite of the 1954 Supreme Court ruling. "If a white man and a Negro wanted to ride in a taxi together, they could not have done so, since by law white operators served white passengers exclusively and Negroes rode in a separate system confined to them."[6] Blacks and whites rode the same buses, but blacks were confined to the back of the bus. In shopping centers, blacks had to wait until all whites had been served. Blacks were not called by the courtesy titles used for whites. All social, professional, and civic organizations in Montgomery were segregated. In fact, King found Montgomery to be segregated in every way.

Birmingham was not unlike Montgomery. In Birmingham, King found that blacks were forced to attend jim crow hospitals and jim crow schools. The white community of Birmingham consistently defied the school desegregation order, and was determined that "blood would run in the streets before desegregation would be permitted to come to Birmingham." Black children played in the streets, because city parks set aside for them were "abysmally inadequate." When a federal court order banned city park segregation, Birmingham gave up its baseball team and closed the parks. In department stores, blacks were allowed to make purchases only at certain counters. It was against the law for blacks to be served food or drink at the same counter with whites. Blacks were not allowed to attend white churches. Although whites professed to be Christian, their churches were as segregated as their theaters, lunch counters, and public parks. When the

Metropolitan Opera toured the South, blacks were not allowed to attend. "The Metropolitan had discontinued scheduling Birmingham on its national tours after it had adopted a policy of not performing before segregated audiences."[7]

That is the Birmingham into which Martin Luther King, Jr., led the civil rights movement. Constant brutality directed against blacks in Birmingham was both unquestioned and unchallenged by the white community. One of the commissioners, Bull Connor, was a racist who took pride in saying he knew how to handle blacks and keep them in their place. The racist white community of Birmingham intimidated, mobbed, and killed many blacks with impunity. A black man was castrated and his mutilated body abandoned on a lonely road. Black homes and churches were bombed. From 1957 through January of 1963, while Birmingham still claimed that its blacks were contented, King reported that seventeen unsolved bombings of black churches and homes of civil rights leaders had occurred.

Theology

Love, Nature of Man, and Nonviolence

King firmly believed that love was the most powerful force in the world. He was much impressed by Ghandi's understanding of love. He said in reference to Ghandi, "The whole concept of 'Satyagraha' (*Satya* is truth which equals love, and *agraha* is force; 'Satyagrapha,' therefore, means truth-force or love force)."[8] He combined this understanding of love with the Christian concept of love and employed it toward social reform. The word that best captures King's understanding of love is *agape*. Agape differs from both *eros* and *philia*. In Platonic philosophy, eros referred to the yearning of the soul for God, but the word has come to mean a sort of romantic love or form of aesthetics. Philia refers to affectionate love between two friends; it is reciprocal love—one loves another and looks for love in return. Agape refers to unconditional or disinterested love; it is unselfish love. Agape does not look for love in return; it doesn't make a distinction between friend and enemy.

King's approach to the nature of the person was very much interrelated to his understanding of love. He felt that human beings have the capacity for good or for evil. Adhering to belief in freedom of the individual, King held that each person must decide which direction he will take in life, whether toward good or toward evil. Since the philosophy of personalism contends that the clue to ultimate reality is found in personality, King developed the principle of the inherent worth and dignity of each individual, and in view of this, he believed there is hope for each individual. Therefore, the task of social reform should not be toward the destruction of the individual but toward the salvation of the individual.

The first principle of nonviolence is that it is not a method for cowards; it does resist, and it is the way of the strong. It employs passive resistance physically and active resistance spiritually. It is nonviolent resistance to evil. The second aspect of nonviolence is that it seeks not to defeat the opponent but to win his friendship and understanding. The nonviolent resister uses such means of protest as noncooperation and boycott to awaken a sense of moral shame in the opponent. A third characteristic of nonviolence is that it takes direct action against the evil itself, and not against the person of the oppressor. King argued that the fight was not between blacks and whites but between the forces of good and evil. He sought to defeat the forces of evil, thus enabling him to win the opponent over, and creating an occasion for reconciliation and redemption. The fourth principle of nonviolence, based on the premise that unearned suffering is redemptive, is that the nonviolent resister must be willing to suffer without retaliation. The final component of nonviolence is that it avoids hate. It seeks not to allow the hatred of the oppressor to infiltrate the mind of the nonviolent resister.

God and Evil

King's conception of God played a dominant role in his courage and faith. He believed that since God was the architect of the universe, the world bends ultimately toward justice, righteousness, and mercy. He thought of evil and injustice not as ultimate, but as merely episodic. He based his theology on the conviction that good eventually will have the final word in reality. Being constantly exposed to all sorts of social evils, King felt the need to believe that God is a God of justice. During his career as a civil rights worker, his life was filled with threats. He said that almost every day someone would warn him they had overheard plans to get rid of him.

During the crisis in Montgomery, these threats against his life greatly disturbed King. Each morning he would look at his family and realize that they could be taken away from him in a moment, and that he could be taken away from them in a moment. He related an experience that increased his faith in God remarkably.

One night, he had settled into bed late, after a long, busy day, but before he dozed off, the telephone rang, and an angry voice said, "Listen, nigger, we've taken all we want from you; before next week you'll be sorry you ever came to Montgomery."[9] Naturally, this incident frightened him very much. He tried to think of a way to move out of the picture without appearing to be a coward. But then he said to God, "I am here taking a stand for what I believe is right. But now I am afraid. The people are looking to me for leadership, and if I stand before them without strength and courage, they too will falter. I am at the end of my powers. I have nothing left. I've come to the point where I can't face it alone."[10]

At that moment, King said he experienced the presence of God unlike anything he had felt before. He heard the quiet assurance of an inner voice saying, "Stand up for righteousness, stand up for truth; and God will be at your side forever."[11] His fears and uncertainty immediately disappeared; he was ready to face anything.

That experience and other similar ones brought King closer to the reality of God's presence in the world. He said that more than ever before, he was convinced of the reality and power of a personal God. In the past, that reality was nothing more than a metaphysical category found in philosophical and theological speculation, but his experiences had made it a living and valid knowledge.

King did not think of evil as illusory or as an error of the modern mind. Rather, he thought of it as having objective reality, but one containing the seeds of its own destruction. He indicated that history is the story of evil forces that had advanced with what appeared to be irresistible power but had been crushed by the forces of justice. "There is a law in the moral world—a silent, invisible imperative, akin to the laws in the physical world—which reminds us that life will work only in a certain way."[12]

He believed that God is able to conquer evil forces. God has placed within the very structure of the universe certain absolute laws, and King argued that man can neither defy nor break those laws. Although the forces of evil may temporarily conquer truth, truth will eventually conquer the conqueror. Here King relies on the words of James Russell Lowell:

Truth forever on the scaffold, Wrong forever on the throne,—
Yet that scaffold sways the future, and, behind the dim unknown,
Standeth God within the shadow, keeping watch above his own.

Christian Hope and the Future
of Black Americans

King's understanding of Christian hope was grounded in the firm conviction that God would set black Americans free in this life. He felt that otherworldly concerns have a deep and important place in Christianity. Christianity, along with other religions, deals not only with man's relationship to his fellow man but also with his relationship to the universe and ultimate reality. "But a religion true to its nature must also be concerned about man's social conditions. Religion deals not only with the hereafter but also with the here."[13]

The struggle for complete justice, love, mercy, and good for all became the focus of King's vision of Christian hope. His desire was to liberate both the oppressed and the oppressors; this would require the elimination of racism and every manner of injustice perpetrated against blacks. Regardless of the degree of oppression, King always articulated hope to the masses. That hope is very evident in his famous address, "I Have a Dream," delivered in 1963, in Washington, D.C.

In spite of the realization that difficult days awaited the civil rights movement, King brought the vision of Christian hope to the people. He said his dream was deeply rooted in the American creed: "We hold these truths to be self-evident, that all men are created equal." His dream was that the children of former slaves and the children of former slave owners in Georgia would be able to work together and to see one another as brothers and sisters. He looked forward to the day when oppressive forces would be defeated, and Mississippi would be transformed into an oasis of freedom and justice. He wanted America to grow in racial consciousness to the extent that people would be judged on the basis of their character and not on their skin color.

When freedom penetrates every level of America, then King said we all will be able to sing with true meaning, "My country, 'tis of thee, sweet land of liberty, of thee I sing. Land where my fathers died, land of the Pilgrim's pride, from every mountainside, let freedom ring." King challenged America to make freedom, justice, goodness, mercy, and love a reality for all people. He felt that accomplishment would be the actualization of the prophecy of Isaiah 40:4, 5. King based his words on that scripture when he said,

> I have a dream that one day every valley shall be exalted,
> every hill and mountain shall be made low.
> The rough places will be made plain,
> and the crooked places will be made straight.
> And the glory of the Lord shall be revealed,
> and all flesh shall see it together.[14]

Contribution

It is hard to measure the depth of Martin Luther King, Jr.'s contributions to humanity. His achievements brought him hundreds of awards and distinctions, and the highest of all honors, the Nobel Peace Prize. He lectured at renowned colleges and universities, preached in outstanding pulpits, and conferred with people from all walks of life. No other single black American has had more impact throughout the world in any generation than Martin Luther King, Jr. He challenged the consciousness of millions of people to come to grips with such noble principles as peace, brotherhood, love, mercy, justice, and goodwill. But what did King feel was his most important contribution?

In a sermon preached at Ebenezer Baptist Church on February 4, 1968, King mentioned what he considered to be his significant contributions to humanity. He said that the important things in his life were not that he was a Nobel Peace Prize Laureate or that he had hundreds of other awards. He didn't feel that where he attended school was important.

The important things in his life, he said, were his constant efforts to serve others—to provide the proper advice to the nation about the war in Vietnam, to feed the hungry, to clothe the naked, and to visit those in prison. He felt that his stands on justice, righteousness, and peace were important. But above all, he felt his greatest contribution was the committed life that he offered to humanity.[15]

King was a noble leader of the masses, but he was not imposed upon them. The Montgomery Improvement Association elected him as their leader, and from the initial Montgomery civil rights struggle, the movement became an international one with King as its chief spokesman. Even so, he never lost touch with the masses from which he had emerged. He marched with them, went to jail with them, prayed with them, was kicked, whipped, and finally killed for the common people.

Throughout his career, King was fortunate to have Coretta Scott King as his wife. When he was elected spokesman for the Montgomery Improvement Association, he did not know what her response would be, because of the possible danger involved, but he found her to be a great source of support. Not only did she encourage him, but she herself became a significant part of the civil rights movement. They marched together and led thousands of black and white civil rights workers, Protestant, Catholic, and Jew, throughout the South, protesting segregation, discrimination, oppression, and all forms of injustice.

King lived a life of dedication and commitment until his death in 1968. He was leading a march in Memphis, Tennessee, on behalf of garbage workers, when he heard again that threats were being made on his life. His response in this instance was different from that in Montgomery at the beginning of the civil rights struggle. In Montgomery, he was beginning his career; in Memphis, he felt that his life was nearing its end. With an undying love for the masses, and with a firm belief that blacks will be free one day, King said,

Well, I don't know what will happen now. We've got some difficult days ahead. But it doesn't matter with me now. Because

MARTIN LUTHER KING, JR. (1929–1968)

I've been to the mountain top. And I don't mind. Like anybody, I would like to live a long life. Longevity has its place. But I'm not concerned about that now. I just want to do God's will. And He's allowed me to go up to the mountain. And I've looked over. And I've seen the promised land. I may not get there with you. But I want you to know tonight that we, as a people, will get to the promised land. And I'm happy tonight. I'm not worried about anything. I'm not fearing any man. Mine eyes have seen the glory of the coming of the Lord.[16]

It would be difficult to mention all the persons who were influenced by King.

Ralph David Abernathy worked very closely with King throughout the entire civil rights movement. King said many times that Abernathy was his closest friend; he helped organize the movement and gave King physical and spiritual support. On countless occasions, Abernathy prayed with him during marches throughout the South; they were jailed together and both suffered much emotional and physical brutality. After the King's death, Abernathy succeeded him as president of the Southern Christian Leadership Conference, a position he resigned not too long afterward. He now commits himself to the fulltime pastorate of Hunter Street Baptist Church in Atlanta.

Another person of national prominence who was much influenced by King is Andrew Young. Although Young was well known during the days of the civil rights struggle, he came to major national attention in 1972, when he launched his campaign for a seat in the United States House of Representatives from Georgia's fifth district. He was the first black elected to Congress from the state of Georgia in over one hundred years. He was reelected in 1974 and 1976. Nominated by President Jimmy Carter, Young became the United States Ambassador to the United Nations on January 30, 1977.

Many of today's leaders, both black and white, worked with King, marched with him, and received the personal benefit of his wisdom, inspiration, and dedication. His followers are functioning in all areas of life as educators, lawyers, physicians, politicians, economists, community organizers, authors, social critics, and in many other occupations.

Chapter XII
Jesse Louis Jackson (1941–   )
*Minister, President of
Operation PUSH*

The life and legacy of Martin Luther King, Jr., have become immortalized on the pages of human history. His leadership has made a major impact on the lives of countless other individuals.

One who worked very closely with King and whom he influenced to a great extent is Jesse Louis Jackson. Jesse Jackson gained national attention when King appointed him national director of Operation Breadbasket in 1967. He continued in that capacity until December, 1971, when he became the founder and national leader of Operation PUSH (People United to Save Humanity).

Early Life and Development

Jesse Jackson was born October 8, 1941, in Greenville, South Carolina. He graduated from Sterling High School in Greenville in 1959 and entered the University of Illinois on a football scholarship. He completed the B.S. degree in sociology at A & T State University in North Carolina. He has received more than twenty-two honorary doctorates from colleges, universities, and seminaries across the country.

Religious Philosophy

Although Jackson admits he has been affected by the religious philosophy of Martin Luther King, Jr., he makes a strong effort to maintain his own creativity, originality, and religious/philosophical self-understanding. Like King, however, Jackson does not remove his religious and philosophical concepts from the arena of social reform; his concern is wholistic and all-inclusive. His involvements begin with the religious concern of spirituality but broaden themselves to include politics, economics, education, and all facets of society.

Jackson challenges blacks to close the gap between where they are, and where they ought to be. In order for blacks to accomplish their potentialities, Jackson points out, they must have strong religious and philosophical values. He indicates that there is no such thing as a value-free people. "Non-values are values, but they are values leading to social, economic and political decadence and decay."[1] Some argue, Jackson contends, that the death of ethics or religious values is the sabotage of excellence. But from his point of view, the black community needs a moral revolution, a revolution in values that will allow it to close the gap. He argues that blacks need a religious philosophy that will enable them to fulfill their essential goals—to be producers, providers, and protectors.

If blacks are to close the gap, Jackson maintains that they must have a philosophy that will empower them to discipline their appetites, engage in sound ethical conduct, and develop their minds. "A steady diet of violence, vandalism, drugs, irresponsible sexual conduct, alcohol and TV addiction has bred a passive, alienated and superficial generation. If the challenge is to close the gap, decadence diverts one from the goal of catching up."[2]

Attempting to encourage many blacks who have succumbed to irresponsible activity and to challenge them to move to a higher level of conceptualization, Jackson points

126

out that a morally weak people not only inhibit their own growth and potential, but they ultimately contribute significantly to the politics of decadence. Just as an intoxicated army cannot fight a war, Jackson says that black minds "full of dope instead of hope will not fight for the right to vote." Blacks as a people must register and vote if they are to move constructively toward closing the gap and achieving their potentials. "A generation lacking the moral and physical stamina necessary to fight a protracted civilizational crisis is dangerous to themselves, their neighbors and future generations. We need a sober, sane, disciplined army to catch up."[3]

Jackson calls upon black and white adults to regain the confidence of this generation's youth. In order to accomplish this necessary task, he says adults need to reestablish a moral authority that represents credibility, trustworthiness, and caring. He feels this will enable the adults to develop and demand discipline in their children, through which they will learn self-discipline.

Philosophy and Ideology

The philosophy and ideology of Jesse Jackson are very much interrelated with that of Operation PUSH, which grew out of Operation Breadbasket, the economic component of the Southern Christian Leadership Conference. As the founder and national director, Jackson shaped the philosophy and ideology of the new organization based on his exposure to and experience with Martin Luther King, Jr., but the substance of the organization's thought and focus was conceived and developed by Jackson himself. The name of the organization, Operation PUSH (People United to Save Humanity), explains its action and goal. The S in PUSH actually stands for two words: Serve–Save. Humanity must be served before it can be saved.

On this point Jackson was tutored by King extremely well; basic to King's entire philosophy and theology was the notion of service. And the element of saving humanity is also basic to King's theological understanding. King's efforts, even until his death, were to save humanity from destruction. King sought not to destroy the oppressor, the evildoer, or the person possessed with wrongful intentions, but through unmerited suffering to reconcile that person. Unlike King, Jackson does not emphasize the various suffering aspects of service and reconciliation.

The philosophy of PUSH is based on the principle that "In the basic struggle for justice and equality . . . the destiny of each of us is tied irrevocably to the destiny of all."[4] Again, this represents a basic theme of King's thought—that "Together we must learn to live as brothers or together we will be forced to perish as fools."[5] The philosophy of PUSH embraces the following programmatic goals:

The right of every able bodied person to get a job at useful work and adequate wages in our expanding peace time economy.

The right of every person to the best medical services available, without dehumanizing ceremony, and regardless of income.

The development and expansion of Black owned and controlled financial/commercial businesses as institutions necessary to a healthy, stable Afro-American survival.

The right of every child to a relevant, quality education, supported by taxation and free of charge, regardless of place of residence.

The right to sanitary, decent housing. The right to secure services from landlords and municipalities which rents and mortgages pay for and are too often discriminately discharged.[6]

Political Philosophy

Jackson has come to the realization that since American society is becoming more and more complex, it is essential that the black community perceive itself and function interdependently with other population groups. He thinks the black vote is becoming much more critical and more necessary in local, state, and national elections. Jackson sees the new competition for the black vote as healthy both for blacks and for the nation. What then is the mutual need? "My fundamental perspective is that *mutual need* is the basis for political alliances. Increasingly, political parties and politicians of all persuasions will have to compete for our vote or risk extinction."[7] Jackson feels that the hope for black political power is pursuit of a strategy that prohibits one party or a component within a party from taking blacks for granted. He encourages blacks to expand their political options and to exhaust the possibilities within both parties.

Jackson maintains that there are at least three political strategies available to blacks.

One option is not to vote. This strategy reflects a cynical point of view which assumes that neither party is working in the interest of black people. While he understands black indifference toward the political process, he argues that nonparticipation only makes matters worse and therefore rejects the "no vote" strategy.

The second option is for blacks to give all their votes to one group of people, based on blind loyalty. Jackson rejects this strategy also, because it gives blacks power but no leverage.

The third option, a more diversified political strategy, and the one Jackson calls for blacks to adopt, is based on vested interest and reciprocity. He says that blacks must exercise all political options open to them, without cynicism, but realistically. At this point, politically speaking, he feels that black people are just like other people. In other words, what is good for black Americans is good for all Americans. "We have never argued for black jobs, but for jobs; never for black housing, but for housing; never for black health care, but for health care. In other words we have never argued for an exclusive or exclusionary political program."[8]

Education Toward Liberation

Jackson developed his philosophy of education around the premise of achievement. The key word that captures his philosophy is "excel." He challenges blacks to excel because of the great educational gap between blacks and whites. He feels genuine education is basic to liberation.

He challenges blacks to excel in education because they do not presently control their share of America. Blacks don't control their share of the nation's business wealth; they don't control their share of physicians; and they are behind in their proportionate number of the nation's engineers, architects, electricians, carpenters, and teachers.

Blacks must excel because there is increased resistance to their upward mobility; racism in America makes it necessary; competition is getting keener; and doors that were once open are now closing.[9]

Jackson's philosophy has culminated in the Operation PUSH concept for excellence in education called EXCEL, based on a premise that calls for total involvement.

Contribution

Within a very short period, Jesse Louis Jackson has become a major force in America. He has been the recipient of several awards, including the 1977 Golden Key Award, an annual award presented by the American Association of School Administrators.

He is a frequent lecturer to high school, college, and professional audiences. He has appeared as guest speaker before more than five hundred groups, including the Democratic National Convention, the Republican National Committee, the Association for the Study of Afro-American Life, the National League of Cities, the National Conference of Mayors, the National Urban League Conference, the United Negro College Fund, and many others.

In association with the Universal syndicate, Jackson writes a column that appears in over seventy-five newspapers nationwide; he was formerly a columnist with the *Los Angeles Times* syndicate.

Jackson's primary emphasis presently is on the development of Operation PUSH, with a focus on the continuing civil economics movement, the improvement of the quality of life of underprivileged and minority groups, and its concept for excellence in education, EXCEL.

In its brief history, PUSH has negotiated and signed major national agreements with such corporations as Schlitz Brewing Company, General Foods Corporation, Quaker Oats Company, and Avon Products, resulting in additional jobs and more opportunity for blacks. The organization has participated in political education and voter registration drives throughout the country and has assisted in various election campaigns. It has established a fulltime community service program that deals with more than twelve thousand complaints annually in the Chicago area. PUSH persuaded the U.S. Department of Housing and Urban Development to declare a moratorium on the foreclosure of multifamily dwellings. It conducted a major food drive for six African nations when their resources were depleted by droughts.

Part V
Black Theology

Chapter XIII
James H. Cone (1938–   )
Minister, Systematic Theologian

One of the most controversial and revolutionary phrases of the 1960s was "black power." It represented a renaissance in the history of black America. Many blacks felt, however, that the era of black power was a giant step backward into the period of segregation and racial hatred. It was their contention that it took years for blacks to become integrated into the mainstream of American life, and that the success they had attained in that direction was far too important to jeopardize with the concept of black power. Some were exponents of the philosophy of universality, which to them transcended ethnic particularization. They wanted to escape identification with the black power slogan and to identify themselves with such concepts as "the individual" and "humanity."

But a large segment of the black community welcomed the idea of black power. To this segment it represented self-determination, self-identity, self-help, and a significant movement toward revolutionary activity. Young black college students throughout the nation responded to the black power theory with great enthusiasm and interest. They, along with many other blacks, were saying that the concept was a step in the right direction, and that if followed through fully, it would enable blacks to establish a firm economic and political base leading to a new approach to integration. They felt that for blacks to attempt to integrate themselves into the mainstream of American life without any sense of power was an illusion. They also felt that for a people to talk meaningfully about such universal ideas as humanity, it was necessary for them to appreciate, respect, and particularize their self-identity. The black power slogan provided the basis for this self-identity.

How did theology respond to the theory?

A young black systematic theologian, James H. Cone, challenged contemporary theology and the church to think seriously about the concept of black power. Graduating from Philander Smith College and Garrett Theological Seminary and receiving the Ph.D. degree in systematic theology in 1965 from Northwestern University, Cone was intellectually prepared for the challenge of developing a liberation theology relevant for black Americans. In 1969, he published his revolutionary *Black Theology and Black Power*, which immediately made him the foremost exponent of black theology in the nation and throughout the world. His popularity and prophetic insights have taken him as guest lecturer to more than one hundred colleges, universities, and seminaries throughout the country, as well as to Europe, Africa, Japan, and South Korea. *Black Theology and Black Power* has been translated into Dutch, German, and Japanese.

Theology

Black Theology and Black Power

In this influential volume, Cone took an affirmative stand on black power, analyzed it from a theological perspective, and attempted to relate it to Christianity, the church, and American theology. He took the position that black power is "Christ's central message to twentieth-century America. And unless the empirical denominational church makes a

133

determined effort to recapture the man Jesus through a total identification with the suffering poor as expressed in Black Power, that church will become exactly what Christ is not."[1] In order that the church remain faithful to God, Cone challenged it to break with the evils of racism and to become prophetic in its message and approach. What then does the Christian message have to say about black power?

Cone was the first to coin the phrase "black theology," representing an effort on his part to appropriate the gospel of Jesus in light of black oppressed existential situations in America. He made it clear that his identity with blackness and its meaning for millions of blacks living in a white society controlled his theological analysis. In this connection, he felt it was impossible for him to surrender the basic reality of blackness for a higher and more universal reality. As he saw it, if a higher ultimate reality is to have meaning, it must relate to the essence of blackness. Using blackness as the point of departure and interpreting it in light of the gospel, Cone pointed out that if the gospel of liberation is for the oppressed, Jesus is wherever the oppressed are continuing his work toward liberation. Because of this, Cone argued, the Christian message is not divergent from black power—it *is* black power!

Cone's central concern in *Black Theology and Black Power* was to demonstrate that the goal and message of black power is consistent with the message of Jesus Christ; if this is the case, Jesus would be an exponent of, and a participant in, the activity of black power. Rather than making a disjunction between theology and black power, Cone employed black power as basic to his interpretation of the Christian faith.

Coming from a community and a people who experienced the forces of racism and oppression daily, Cone sought to substantiate the social activism among blacks in the 1960s and subsequent years in a theological context. His theological position represented a marriage between the black church and the black community. Many black college students during the 60s were very critical of the black church for not being significantly involved in the liberation struggle. Cone's theological position helped greatly to overcome this gap. To follow his position would put the black church on the cutting edge of the liberation struggle. He argued that black theology was an earthly theology not concerned with heaven or the "last things," but with the white situation in America. In this sense, Cone challenged all segments of the black community, including the church, to involve themselves in the liberation struggle.

Since Cone used blackness as the point of departure in constructing his theology, how do whites fit into the picture? Do they have any way to be reconciled to blacks? Cone answered this by saying that "being black in America has very little to do with skin color. To be black means that your heart, your soul, your mind, and your body are where the dispossessed are."[2] With the realization that America will threaten a black man in white skin just as quickly as it will threaten a black man in black skin, Cone said that being reconciled to God does not mean that one's skin has to become physically black; the important thing, he felt, is the color of one's heart, soul, and mind.

A Black Theology of Liberation

The importance of Cone's *Black Theology and Black Power* to this generation of blacks and whites cannot be overemphasized. Even so, it was merely a prolegomenon to a fuller, more substantive, and more comprehensive development of black theology. Cone had planted the seeds that took shape in a later work, *A Black Theology of Liberation*, published in 1970. Here he sets forth more systematically the fundamental issues related to his discussion.

Cone begins with the conviction that Christian theology is a theology of liberation. "It is a rational study of the being of God in the world in light of the existential situation of an oppressed community, relating the forces of liberation to the essence of the gospel, which is Jesus Christ."[3] Here he delineates the focus of theology—it must concern itself with the poor, dispossessed, and suffering. To further support his claim, Cone identifies the theme of liberation from oppression throughout the biblical record. Cone argues that historically, God identified himself with the poor and oppressed of the land. It follows then that in order for theology to be genuine and Christian, it must identify itself with the poor and dispossessed. This makes black theology a theology of liberation because it arises from an identification with the oppressed black Americans. Black theology attempts to interpret the gospel of Christ in light of the existential situation of blacks and adheres to the position that the liberation of blacks in America is God's intention.

Cone feels there are two fundamental reasons why black theology is Christian theology and is possibly the only expression of Christian theology in America. The first reason is that there can be no theology of the gospel of Christ which does not arise from the oppressed. The second is that black theology centers itself on Jesus Christ. Although Cone affirms the black experience as basic in developing black theology, he is careful not to minimize the importance of Jesus Christ as not only the norm and point of departure for black theology but also as the foundation of all Christian theology.

The Sources and Norm for Black Theology

Some critics misunderstood the thrust of Cone's theology in his earlier book, *Black Theology and Black Power.* Because of his heavy emphasis on the themes of "liberation" and "black power," these critics argued that he substituted these themes for Jesus Christ as the norm for black theology. Some felt that Cone was developing a religion of black power rather than a black theology. As a highly trained and skilled systematic theologian, however, Cone was careful not to fall guilty to that charge. Jesus

136

Christ is operative as the norm for black theology in all his books, but Cone seeks to formulate his understanding more systematically in *A Black Theology of Liberation.*

In James Cone's view, it is very important not to confuse the sources of black theology with the norm. Those sources are the black experience, black history, black culture, revelation, scripture, and tradition. These constitute significant experiences within the black community, which Cone feels are essential for constructing a black theology. For him, theology is not done in abstraction and is not removed from community experience. He feels that theology grows out of the community, and the theologian seeks to criticize, interpret, and analyze community experiences in light of God-talk. On this basis he interprets the sources of black theology from the perspective of the black community.

An understanding of God-talk in black theology must begin with an understanding of the black experience and history as the point of departure. Black cultural expressions are necessary in order to make God-talk relevant and meaningful to the black community. The question of revelation within the context of black theology, Cone argues, is not just a question of a past or contemporary event in which the activity of God is difficult to discern; in black theology, revelation is a black event. It represents what blacks are doing about their liberation. As the Bible points beyond itself to the reality of God's activity in the world, Cone interprets scripture in the light of black liberation. When he speaks of tradition, Cone focuses primarily on the history of the black church in America. He feels that such historic black figures as Richard Allen, Henry Highland Garnet, and David Alexander Payne, rather than Luther, Calvin, and Wesley, are basic for an interpretation of black liberation.

Not only does he ground the sources of black theology in Jesus Christ as the norm, Cone also contends that "it is not possible to speak meaningfully to the black community about liberation unless it is analyzed from a Christian perspective which centers on Jesus Christ."[4] Cone now moves toward a more fully developed Christology. He says that Christian theology begins and ends with Jesus Christ as the point of departure for everything said about God, man, and the world. But what meaning does Christ have in the context of black theology?

Cone places much emphasis on the historical Jesus in an attempt to make Christ relevant and meaningful to the black condition in America. In order to know who Jesus is, Cone feels that we must know who he was. "Without some continuity between the historical Jesus and the kerygmatic Christ, the Christian gospel becomes nothing but the subjective reflections of the early Christian community."[5] Cone believes that the historical Jesus as portrayed in the New Testament is an oppressed person, one who in his earthly existence identified himself with the oppressed of the land. For Cone, the identification of the historical Jesus with the oppressed is decisive and should be reflected in both historic and contemporary interpretations of Jesus Christ.

God of the Oppressed

James Cone's work, God of the Oppressed, published in 1975, is a yet more comprehensive development of his thought. His earlier works, Black Theology and Black Power, A Black Theology of Liberation, and The Spirituals and the Blues, all culminated in God of the Oppressed. Cone is consistent throughout his writings. Although they clearly show a progression in his thought, he has maintained the theological position taken in his earlier books. In Black Theology and Black Power, he attempted to demonstrate the relevance of the Christian message to black power. His theological position was expanded and further systematically formulated in A Black Theology of Liberation. His emphasis in God of the Oppressed is primarily concerned with the particular and the universal. His main thesis is that "one's social and historical context decides not only the questions we address to God but also the mode or form of the answers given to the questions."[6]

Cone's doctrine is grounded in the biblical tradition and the black experience. He views God as the primary reality who is fighting actively against racism and oppression. God, then, elected, or chose, blacks as his own. He chose blacks, Cone feels, not for redemptive suffering, but for freedom. Cone does not view blacks as elected by God to be his suffering servants. Rather, they were elected by God for freedom because they are oppressed, against their will and against God's. Therefore, God has decided to make their quest for liberation his own.

Cone identifies as God's first fight in the cause of liberation his deliverance of the Israelites from oppression in Egypt. He contends that God elected Israel to be liberated from the forces of bondage and oppression; and throughout both the Old and the New Testaments, God identified himself with the cause of liberation. In contemporary America, Cone feels that the treatment of blacks represents the worst form of oppression. Because God historically has identified himself with those who were oppressed, Cone argues that God has elected blacks to participate in this struggle. Based on this understanding, Cone feels that for theology or God-talk to be Christian, it must identify itself with the oppressed.

Following the logic of this argument, Cone points out that "God himself must be known only as he reveals himself in his blackness. The blackness of God, and everything implied by it in a racist society, is the heart of Black Theology's doctrine of God."[7] Cone doesn't feel there is any place in black theology for a colorless God, since blacks suffer because of their color. Does this mean that God is a God for blacks only, or for all peoples? Cone begins with the particularization of God-talk, showing that God identifies himself with blackness and rejects whiteness. Here it is important to note in what context Cone uses the words "black" and "white."

There are two definitions of blackness in Cone's thought. First, he uses blackness as a physiological trait. In this sense, it refers to a particular black-skinned people in America and elsewhere, who have been victimized by oppression and racism. These people, Cone believes, are the key to Christian theology and divine revelation. Second, Cone uses blackness as an ontological symbol to refer to all people who participate in the struggle for liberation. This is the universal aspect of Cone's theological program. Based on the historic reality of oppression, racism, and cruelty, Cone interprets whiteness to represent the Antichrist and those evil forces working against God's cause of liberation. To escape this condemnation, Cone challenges whites to join God's fight for the cause of black liberation.

Because God has made the cause of black liberation his own, Cone feels that his doctrine of God should begin with insistence on God's blackness. " 'How can white people become black?' is analogous to the Philippian jailer's question to Paul and Silas, 'What must I do to be saved?' "[8] According to Cone, to be saved, whites must accept blackness, because blackness and salvation are synonymous. In this sense God as the wholly other has come in his blackness, which is wholly unlike whiteness; and to receive God's divine revelation, Cone contends, one must become black with God.

Not only does Cone view God as black, but he also thinks of Christ as black, both literally and symbolically. Christ's blackness is literal in the sense that he truly identifies himself with the oppressed blacks; Christ takes the suffering of blacks as his own suffering. The blackness of Christ means that blacks are God's oppressed people whom Christ has come to liberate. It denotes also that God in his infinite wisdom has disclosed himself for redemption through the blood of the black Christ. Therefore, the blackness of Christ indicates more than skin color; it is the transcendent affirmation that God has never forsaken the oppressed.

Contribution

The black theology of James H. Cone has been a milestone in contemporary theological discourse. Regardless of whether or not one agrees with his position, one would have to admit that it is indeed prophetic, revolutionary, and penetrating. He gave birth to the idea of black theology in contemporary America, although he would be the first to admit that black theology is not new, because its roots can be found in black religion. But the concept and systemic formulation of black theology originated with James H. Cone.

With the publication of *Black Theology and Black Power*, the ideas of James Cone shook the foundations of theological seminaries, colleges, and universities throughout the country and the world. These institutions of higher learning began to consider the black religious experience more seriously, courses in black theology were organized and taught in many seminaries, and many black scholars were recruited to teach such courses. The thought of James Cone was not the only prophetic voice operative in challenging whites to take notice of the black presence, but it was, and indeed remains, a significant voice.

Many scholars—black and white, ministers and laypersons—have been influenced by Cone's thought. His convictions represent the seed of much liberation theology that is discussed today in America and Europe. He was one of the earliest theologians to launch a program around the theme of liberation. Cone's thought influenced Frederick Herzog, professor of systematic theology at Duke Divinity School, in the content of his *Liberation Theology*. He believed Cone's challenge that whites must become black in order to be "saved." In a hermeneutical analysis of the third chapter of John, Herzog argued essentially the same thesis developed by James Cone—that whites must negate all forms of racism and oppression and take heed of God's call to liberation.

Responding to open presentations at a symposium on Hope and the Future of Man, held in New York City in October, 1971, and attended by many leading theologians, Jürgen Moltmann argued, "Liberal theology no longer grips me. Only *liberation theology* is for me a theology which radically focuses on Christian hope, as it has been proposed in this country by James H. Cone and Frederick Herzog."[9] Moltmann's contention was that without a transformation of the inhuman system in which blacks and other poor people are the victims of oppression, there will be no future for humanity. He contended in agreement with both men that "a hope which is not the hope of the oppressed today is no hope for which I could give a theological account."[10]

Peter C. Hodgson of Vanderbilt Divinity School also showed Cone's influence in both his *Children of Freedom* and his *New Birth of Freedom: A Theology of Bondage and Liberation.*

Chapter XIV
J. Deotis Roberts, Sr. (1927–   )
Minister, Philosophical
Theologian

Whenever a major theological position is advanced, there is always someone to take it to task. No position, regardless of how influential, is immune to criticism and/or the need for further development. There is no such thing as a definitive theological system; although some individuals dominate theological discourse for a period, their systems eventually exhaust themselves and pave the way for new, more creative thinkers to emerge.

Such major figures as Immanuel Kant, Friedrich Daniel Schleiermacher, Friedrich Hegel, Karl Marx, Ludwig Feuerbach, Ernst Troeltsch, Adolf Harnack, and Sören Kierkegaard dominated early twentieth-century American theology. But with the publication of Karl Barth's *Epistle to the Romans*, the liberal theology of the nineteenth century greatly lost its impact, and there emerged a new understanding of God and man. This new theological understanding, known as neoorthodox, held sway until Paul Tillich developed an influential system and criticized Barth in several areas. Barth, a kerygmatic theologian, dealt with the unchanging eternal truths of God, while Tillich, a systematic theologian, dealt with relating those eternal truths to the forever-changing human predicament.

When J. Deotis Roberts, Sr., published *Liberation and Reconciliation: A Black Theology* in 1971 as a critique of James H. Cone's theological program, it represented the first major attempt to take Cone to task. Although Cone and Roberts are both technically trained black theologians, they represent two different schools of thought. James Cone received his Ph.D. in systematic theology from Northwestern University and his dissertation was on Karl Barth. His study in the New Testament accounts for his heavy emphasis on the biblical tradition in formulating his theological program. Roberts earned his Ph.D. at the University of Edinburgh in Scotland and wrote his dissertation on "The Rational Theology of Benjamin Whichcote: Father of the Cambridge Platonists."

Early Life and Development

J. Deotis Roberts, Sr., has had a rich and diversified career in the area of theology. He was born in Spindate, North Carolina, on July 12, 1927, and was educated at Johnson C. Smith University, Shaw University, Hartford Seminary Foundation, and the University of Edinburgh. He did further study at Cambridge University and has held major study fellowships from the Lilly Foundation, the Ford Foundation, and the Association of Theological Scholars. Those fellowships have enabled him to examine many religions, traveling to numerous countries in Europe, Asia, and Africa, and also to study at Harvard Divinity School, Duke University, the University of Chicago, and Michigan State University.

Roberts' concern during his study-travels has been in the area of comparative religions. He maintains an interest in the broad scope of religion and endeavors to understand it in the context of both its particularity and its universality. As a result of this wide exposure to other religious traditions and his theological orientation, Roberts seeks to develop a black theology from a more inclusive perspective than did James Cone.

J. DEOTIS ROBERTS, SR. (1927–)

Theology

Liberation and Reconciliation

One of Roberts' persistent criticisms of theologians is that they have been too generous toward Cone. He feels that before his own book was published in 1971, Cone's theological program had escaped constructive criticism. He accuses white theologians of being perhaps indifferent toward Cone. In some cases, he thinks whites have used Cone as a "straw man," in order to ignore all other black theologians, with the intention of rejecting black theology altogether. He says both black and white theologians have had only skirmishes with James Cone.[1]

In *Liberation and Reconciliation: A Black Theology*, Roberts attempted to provide what he considered a missing link in Cone's theological program—reconciliation. Roberts' contention is that "liberation and reconciliation are the two main poles of Black Theology. They are not antithetical—one moves naturally from one to the other in the light of the Christian understanding of God and man."[2] He feels there is a theological basis for reconciliation "between equals," but he thinks that reconciliation is postrevolutionary in its ultimate direction. Roberts is calling for a revolution in race relations with reconciliation as an essential component.

By reconciliation in race relations between equals, Roberts means that in the struggle for black liberation, whites no longer can be lieutenants but must be demoted to buck privates in the black community. He accepts Cone's contention that whites must allow blacks to set the rules for the liberation struggle. He says, "Cone is correct—only the oppressed may write the agenda for their liberation." He calls for whites to engage themselves more in their own communities, preparing their neighbors to accept blacks as a people in a pluralistic society. Roberts insists that blacks and whites, acting through vigorous protest, speaking and moving through the black church and the black community, can spark the revolution that liberates all blacks from the forces of oppression. But beyond liberation or the revolution, Roberts contends, there must be a blueprint for a true Christian reconciliation. He doesn't feel that reconciliation should be dealt with in a futuristic manner. He said, "We reply to our critics that in the nature of our faith we must always seek reconciliation. Christianity is rooted in the belief that 'God was in Christ reconciling the world to himself.' (II Cor. 5:19)."[3]

Black scholars who adhered to a more moderate stance welcomed the theological program of Roberts as a relief from the dogmatic approach of James Cone. More militant-minded scholars, however, rejected Roberts' position as too moderate and not in keeping with the immediate theological demands of the black revolution. Still, a close examination of Cone's thought reveals that he has always included the element of reconciliation. In this sense, his thought has not been as one-sided as many of his critics have argued. But the problem for Roberts and others has been the terms of Cone's program of reconciliation, which begins and ends with blackness as the key to divinity. He begins with blackness as a physiological trait and ends with blackness as an ontological model. It is within the context of this model that Cone's understanding of reconciliation exists. When whites identify themselves authentically with black oppression, they become black ontologically, or symbolically.

Having been exposed to comparative religions, Roberts seeks to make the element of universality in the Christian faith inclusive and colorless. Thus, for Roberts, whites do not have to become "black" to be reconciled with blacks, but they must "accept blacks as equals." In this way, Roberts seeks to protect the integrity and humanity of both blacks and whites. Whites commit inhuman acts against blacks which Roberts calls sin, but he feels that a revolution would alter this situation and create a genuine feeling of equality between blacks and whites in a postrevolutionary situation, which he categorizes as reconciliation. Cone negated "whiteness" as evil and sinful, meaning that for whites to be "saved," they must negate themselves and become the "wholly other" of God, which is blackness. Roberts, however, feels that "the assertion that all are 'one in Christ Jesus' must henceforth mean that all slave/master, servant/boss, inferior/superior frames of reference between blacks and whites have been abolished." This principle, he feels, must function not only on the spiritual level but also on the level of social relations. This means not only that blacks—the ex-slaves—must be set free, but that the slave system itself must be abolished. "Reconciliation between equals, no less than liberation, is the mission of the black church."[4]

The Black Man's God

Roberts feels that the task of black theology is to relate God-talk to the hard realities of the captives of the slums, the residents of the dark ghetto, the sharecroppers, the "other Americans," and those who live on the other side of the tracks. The problem of racism in America is the common denominator that brings all blacks together. There is no escape. Whether a black person is rich or poor, the experience of racism is inevitable. Roberts points out that blacks who have good jobs, who live in clean neighborhoods, who are well-traveled, educated, and cultured are not free either. "In the face of the reality of racism in America, the revelation of God to the black poor is equally valid, in most cases, to the black bourgeoisie."[5] What then is God's revelatory message to blacks in America?

Roberts contends that God's revelation is both personal and social; it is both existential and political. It combines spirituality and social reality. It concerns itself with material as well as heavenly things. The context of God's revelation includes the physical/spiritual dimensions consistent with the human body/spirit nature and is directed to the whole person. It reaches into the depth of his personal existence. It is also directed toward those environmental conditions that tend to oppress humanity. God's revelation to blacks "is a revelation of Black Power, which includes black awareness, black pride, black self-respect, and a desire to determine one's own destiny."[6]

The concept of power is very important to blacks, who are essentially powerless. Since black theology addresses itself to these people, Roberts feels the idea of God's omnipotence is of crucial importance. He says that what is needed to inspire faith in those who are constantly experiencing oppression is a belief in an all-powerful God who can defeat the oppressors and bring justice.

The Black Messiah

Roberts is very clear in indicating that he doesn't take the figure of a black Messiah in a literal historical sense. Rather, he sees the "Black Messiah" as a symbol or a myth with deep meaning for black oppressed people. Roberts' concern is psychological. He attempts to particularize God's redemptive act in Jesus Christ in light of the fact that Christ needs to speak to blacks in their particular situation. But how can Christ do this effectively and at the same time maintain his universality? Here is where Roberts differs radically from Cone.

Roberts argues that a universal Christ would be as existentially meaningful to red, yellow, and white peoples as he would be to black. He says that one reason he resists the idea of a black Christ, to the exclusion of a white Christ, is that this would automatically exclude the possibility of a yellow- or other-colored Christ who could confront humanity in other historical-cultural situations. Cone argues to the contrary—that the black Christ ontologically stands as the paradigmatic model for all people to see the activity of God in the contemporary situation. Roberts feels that to portray Christ as black would militate against his relevance and meaningfulness for other oppressed peoples—those peoples of the Third World who are not black but who need a christological symbol for liberation as much as blacks do. He points out that many oppressed peoples are not in Africa or America, but are in Asia, Latin America, and other parts of the globe. Because of this, "If we give our Christology the right shape, we may be helpful in making Christ the 'Desire of all nations.' In one sense Christ must be said to be universal and therefore colorless."[7] Thus, it is only within the context of a mythical image, Roberts feels, that we should perceive Christ as the Black Messiah.

As a mythical image, the black Christ participates in the black experience. Christ makes contact with the black community and relates himself to the unique history and personal experience of blacks. Blacks confront Christ in their experience; at the same time, Roberts contends, this confrontation with the Black Messiah, who is also the universal Christ, points them beyond mere symbolism. "The universal Christ is particularized for the black Christian in the black experience of the black Messiah, but the black Messiah is at the same time universalized in the Christ of the Gospels who meets all men in their situation. The *black Messiah* liberates the black man. The universal Christ *reconciles* the black man with the rest of mankind."[8]

Contribution

J. Deotis Roberts has added a much-needed dimension to black theology and continues to do so. An upcoming collection of essays on contextualization and liberation in Third World theologies, as well as black theology, is due to be published by Orbis Books in 1979. This volume will show Roberts' continuing interest in particularity and universality. His abiding concern with black theology is equalled by his interest in relating the struggle of black Americans to that of all oppressed peoples. This is evidenced by his recent lecture series on African and black theologies at Marburg and Tubingen, Germany.

Roberts established himself as a first-rate theologian prior to his interest in black theology. His master's thesis at Hartford Seminary was published in 1962 under the title *Faith and Reason in Bergson and James*. His major study, *From Puritanism to Platonism in Seventeenth Century England*, was also published in 1962. He has written many articles in scholarly journals, and has been guest lecturer and visiting professor at many of the leading colleges, universities, and seminaries throughout America. The greatest portion of his theological career has been at Howard University School of Religion, where he has been professor of history of philosophy of religion and theology for several years. He is also editor of the *Journal of Religious Thought*.

Conclusion

The contemporary black church has inherited a great tradition of involvement in every segment of the black community. Only through a clear understanding and appreciation of this tradition can black religious leaders develop viable models of ministry for the future. The discussion of representative thinkers both in *Major Black Religious Leaders: 1755–1940* and in this volume attempts to establish clearly a link between the past and present styles of leadership in the black church. These volumes reveal that this leadership in its historic and contemporary circumstances has been focused toward the achievement of freedom and liberation for blacks in America. Black religious leaders have always known that if blacks are to be liberated, the social, political, educational, economic, and cultural institutional structures must be reformed. Blacks could not afford to have a style of ministry dealing exclusively with the spiritual dimensions of existence. Nor could they wait for other institutions to take the initiative toward the achievement of liberation. These leaders discovered very early that if blacks are to be free, the black church must become proactive, rather than reactive.

As opposed to having a reactive posture to social injustices, black religious leaders must provide direction for the black church to be proactive in self-determination, self-sufficiency, and economic, educational, cultural, and political development. The future of the black church is dependent to a great extent upon its capacity to deal effectively with these forever-changing social conditions that plague the black community. In order for the black church to maintain its historic centrality, it must take the lead in interpreting the religious and social dimensions in the black community and find meaningful models of ministry to deal significantly with them.

In order for black religious leaders to provide direction for the black church, they must have a clear understanding of the church's purpose and mission in the world. Both volumes of this study demonstrate that the black church has always had a decompartmentalized theological orientation, meaning that it interprets religious dimension in light of its interrelatedness with the social, political, economic, educational, and cultural aspects of existence. From a wholistic perspective, black religious leaders have integrated the religious and social dimensions of existence into a functional approach to social reform. The purpose and mission of the black church must be constantly redefined and restructured in light of new and changing conditions. What is black religious leadership doing to assist the black church in redefining its purpose and mission?

This question was answered in "The Statement of the National Committee of Black Churchmen on the Urban Mission in a Time of Crisis":

In order to prepare black churches to better serve the communities in which they exist, the National Committee of Black Churchmen commits itself to the development of a new and creative style of black churchmanship which will emphasize its distinctive task and opportunity. There are three interrelated dimensions for this new style of mission:

(1) The renewal and enhancement of the black church in terms of its liturgical life, its theological life, its theological interpreta-

152

tion, its understanding of its mission to itself, to the white church and to the nation.

(2) The development of the black church, not only as a religious fellowship but as a community organization . . . which uses its resources, influence and manpower to address the problems of estrangement, resignation and powerlessness in the political, cultural and economic life of the black community.

(3) The projection of a new quality of church life which would equip and strengthen the church as custodian and interpreter of that cultural heritage which is rooted in the peculiar experience of black people in the United States and the faith that has sustained them for over two centuries on these shores.[1]

What are some of the social conditions presently facing black religious leaders and the black church? Crime is one major crisis. The rate of homicide within the black community is increasing at an unprecedented pace. What are the sociological, psychological, and theological conditions related to the growing problem of crime? To deal effectively with this problem requires a wholistic approach, since the causal factors are complex and interrelated. But what style of religious leadership is needed? And what programs should the black church develop in this regard? How does the problem of crime in the black community fit into the purpose and mission of the black church?

Most major cities in America are becoming predominately black in population. As a result, blacks in the inner cities throughout the country are experiencing declining quality and quantity of housing, education, health care, welfare services, vocational opportunities, and community facilities. They are experiencing high rates of unemployment. How do these problems fit into the purpose and mission of the black church? How can black religious leaders adjust their styles of leadership to be more effective in dealing with these problems?

It is my contention that black religious leaders and the black church must be proactive in attempting to resolve these problems, and must find new ways to make the spiritual dimension of existence effective in resolving malfunctions within the social, political, economic, educational, and cultural segments of the black community.

Notes

Introduction

1. Henry J. Young, *Major Black Religious Leaders: 1755–1940* (Nashville: Abingdon, 1977), p. 15.

Chapter I

1. W. E. B. DeBois, *The Souls of Black Folk* (Connecticut: Fawcett Publications, 1961).

2. *The Autobiography of W. E. B. DuBois* (New York: International Publishers, 1968), p. 147.

3. DuBois, *Dusk of Dawn* (New York: Schocken Books, 1968), pp. 85, 86.

4. *Autobiography*, p. 428.

5. DuBois, *Dark Water* (New York: Harcourt, Brace & Co., 1920), p. 25. Portions of "A Litany of Atlanta" are reprinted by permission of David Graham DuBois.

6. Ibid., pp. 25, 26, 27.

7. Ibid.

8. Ibid., p. 27.

9. Ibid.

10. DuBois, *The Souls of Black Folk*, p. 189.

11. Ibid., p. 17.

12. E. Franklin Frazier, *The Negro Church in America* (New York: Schocken Books, 1963), p. 6.

13. Introduction, *The Souls of Black Folk*, p. ix.

14. *Autobiography*, pp. 431-40.

Chapter II

1. Mordecai Wyatt Johnson, "The Negro and His Relationships," Proceedings of the National Conference of Social Work (University of Chicago Press, 1937), pp. 56-70.

2. August Meier, Elliott Rudwick, and Francis L. Broderick, eds., *Black Protest Thought in the Twentieth Century* (New York: Bobbs-Merrill, 1965), pp. xxiv-xxv.

3. Inaugural Address of Mordecai Wyatt Johnson, President, Howard University, June Tenth, Nineteen Twenty-Seven, *Education for Freedom*, Moorland-Spingarn Research Center, Washington, D.C., 1976, pp. 23, 24.

4. Johnson, "The Faith of the American Negro" in *Negro Orators and Their Orations*, Carter G. Woodson, ed. (New York: Russell & Russell, 1969), pp. 658-60.

5. Johnson, Inaugural Address, p. 30.

6. "A Brief Glimpse at a Great Future," p. 2. Address delivered by Johnson, March 27, 1938, in Cleveland, Ohio; Moorland-Spingarn Collection, Howard University.

7. Johnson, Inaugural Address, p. 28.

8. Ibid., p. 29.

9. *Chronicle of Higher Education* (July 17, 1978), p. 7.

10. Lerone Bennett, *What Manner of Man* (Chicago: Johnson Publishing Co., 1968), p. 37.

Chapter III
1. Benjamin Elijah Mays, *Born to Rebel* (New York: Charles Scribner's Sons, 1971).

2. Ibid., pp. 35, 2.

3. Benjamin E. Mays and Joseph W. Nicholson, *The Negro's Church* (New York: Institute of Social and Religious Research, 1933), p. 281.

4. Ibid., pp. 278-86.

5. Mays, "The Church and the Development of Black Leadership in America." (Paper delivered at University of Tennessee, Knoxville, Tennessee, February 20, 1978), p. 6.

6. Ibid., p. 8.

7. Ibid., p. 11.

8. Mays, *Born to Rebel*, p. 36.

9. Mays, *The Negro's God*, (New York: Atheneum, 1968), pp. 1-8.

10. Mays, "The Development of Black Leadership," pp. 11, 12.

11. Mays, *Disturbed About Man* (Richmond, Va.: John Knox Press, 1969), p. 91.

12. Paul Tillich, *Systematic Theology* (Chicago: University of Chicago Press, 1971).

13. *Disturbed About Man*, p. 92.

14. Ibid., pp. 93-97.

15. Mays, "Conquering Faith," *Preaching the Gospel*, Henry James Young, ed. (Philadelphia: Fortress Press, 1976), p. 35.

16. *Disturbed About Man*, p. 69.

17. Introduction, *Born to Rebel*, p. xvii.

Chapter IV
1. *Common Ground: Essays in Honor of Howard Thurman*, Samuel L. Gandy, ed. (Washington: Haffman Press, 1976), Foreword.

2. Thurman, *The Luminous Darkness* (New York: Harper & Row, 1965), p. 66.

3. Thurman, *The Search for Common Ground* (New York: Harper & Row, 1971), p. 4.

4. Ibid., p. 5.

5. Ibid., p. 25.

6. Thurman, *Deep River* (New York: Kennikat Press, 1945), pp. 55, 56.

7. Ibid., p. 60.

8. Ibid., pp. 61, 62.

9. Thurman, *Jesus and the Disinherited* (Nashville: Abingdon Press, 1945), p. 11.

10. Ibid., p. 28.

Chapter V

1. Adam Clayton Powell, Jr., *Adam by Adam: The Autobiography of Adam Clayton Powell, Jr.* (New York: Dial Press, 1971), p. 27.

2. Ibid., p. 34.

3. *Autobiography*, p. 37.

4. Ibid., p. 43.

5. Ibid., p. 42.

6. Ibid., p. 40.

7. Ibid., p. 39.

8. Ibid.

9. Powell, "My Black Position Paper," *The Black Power Revolt*, Floyd B. Barbour, ed. (Canada: Collier-Macmillan, 1969), pp. 305-9; from the *Congressional Record*, 89th Congress, 2nd session.

10. David Hapgood, *The Purge That Failed: Tammany V. Powell* (New York: Henry Holt and Company, 1959), pp. 1-15.

11. Andy Jacobs, *The Powell Affair* (New York: Bobbs-Merrill, 1973), pp. 237-55.

Chapter VI

1. C. Eric Lincoln, *The Black Muslims in America* (Boston: Beacon Press, 1963), p. xv.

2. Foreword, Elijah Muhammad, *Message to the Blackman in America* (Chicago: Muhammad Mosque of Islam No. 2, 1965), pp. xiii-xiv.

3. Muhammad, *Message to the Blackman*, pp. 20-24.

4. Ibid.

5. Ibid., p. 29.

6. Ibid., p. 31.

7. Ibid., p. 53.

8. Ibid., p. 68.

Chapter VII

1. Alex Haley, *The Autobiography of Malcolm X* (New York: Ballantine Books, 1965), p. 2.

2. Ibid., p. 29.

3. Ibid., p. 191.

4. Ibid., p. 199.

5. Ibid., p. 212.

6. *The End of White Supremacy: Four Speeches by Malcolm X*, Benjamin Goodman, ed. (New York: Merlin House, 1971), pp. 121-48.

7. *Autobiography*, p. 305.

8. Ibid., p. 301.

9. Ibid., p. 321.

10. Ibid., p. 345.

11. Ibid., pp. 345, 346.

12. Malcolm X, "Letters from Mecca," *The Black Power Revolt*, Floyd B. Barbour, ed. (New York: P. F. Collier, 1968), p. 289.

13. George Breitman, *The Last Year of Malcolm X* (New York: Schocken Books, 1967), pp. 112-24.

Chapter VIII

1. Albert Cleage, Jr., *The Black Messiah* (New York: Sheed & Ward, 1968), p. 3.

2. Ibid., p. 7.

3. Ibid., p. 8.

4. Cleage, *Black Christian Nationalism* (New York: William Morrow & Co., 1972), p. 67.

5. Ibid., p. 76.

Chapter IX

1. C. Eric Lincoln, *The Black Church Since Frazier* (New York: Schocken Books, 1974), p. 106.

2. Lincoln, "Contemporary Black Religion: In Search of a Sociology." (Paper delivered at North Carolina Central University, February 6, 1978), p. 4.

3. Ibid., p. 3.

4. Ibid., p. 15.

5. Lincoln, "Americanity: The Third Force in American Pluralism," *Religious Education* (Sept./Oct. 1975), p. 485.

6. Lincoln, "The Racial Factor in the Shaping of American Religion." (Paper delivered at Vassar College, November 9, 1977), p. 1.

7. Ibid., p. 9.

Chapter X

1. Charles Shelby Rooks, "From Genesis to Revelation—Black Identity in the Church," *Shawensis* (Summer 1969), p. 30.

2. Rooks, "The Minister as a Change Agent," *The Journal of the Interdenominational Theological Center* (Fall 1977), pp. 12, 13.

3. Ibid., p. 17.

4. Ibid., p. 22.

5. Ibid.

6. Ibid., p. 23.

7. Rooks, "First Dozen Years Àre the Hardest," *The Journal of the Interdenominational Theological Center* (Fall 1973), pp. 95, 96.

8. Ibid.

9. Rooks, "Theological Education and the Black Church," *The Christian Century* (February 12, 1969), p. 212.

10. Ibid.

11. Marvin J. Taylor, ed., *Fact Book on Theological Education 1977–78* (Vandalia, Ohio: Association of Theological Schools), pp. 7, 8.

12. Rooks, "Implications of the Black Church for Theological Education," *The Voice* (January 1969), p. 5.

Chapter XI

1. Benjamin E. Mays, *Disturbed About Man* (Richmond: John Knox Press, 1969), p. 14.

2. Lerone Bennett, *What Manner of Man?* (Chicago: Johnson Publishing Co., 1968), p. 27.

3. Martin Luther King, Jr., *Stride Toward Freedom* (New York: Harper & Brothers, 1958), p. 80.

4. Ibid., pp. 74, 75.

5. L. Harold DeWolf, "Martin Luther King, Jr. as Theologian," *The Journal of the Interdenominational Theological Center* (Spring 1977), p. 8.

6. *Stride Toward Freedom*, pp. 10-27.

7. King, *Why We Can't Wait* (New York: Signet, 1964), pp. 40-58.

8. *Stride Toward Freedom*, p. 78.

9. Ibid., p. 109.

10. Ibid.

11. Ibid., p. 115.

12. King, *Strength to Love* (New York: Harper & Row, 1963), p. 103.

13. King, "A Challenge to the Churches and Synagogues," *Challenge to Religion*, Mathew Ahmann, ed. (Chicago: Henry Regnery Co., 1963), p. 157.

14. King, "I Have a Dream." Address at Washington, D.C., August 28, 1963, pp. 1-7.

15. King, "Drum Major Instinct," *Preaching the Gospel*, Henry James Young, ed. (Philadelphia: Fortress Press, 1976), pp. 40-45.

16. King, "I've Been to the Mountain Top." Address in Memphis, Tennessee, April 3, 1968.

Chapter XII

1. Jesse Louis Jackson, "In Pursuit of Equity, Ethics and Excellence: The Challenge to Close the Gap." Address to the PUSH/HEW/Howard University National Conference on Excellence, May 17, 1978, pp. 9, 10.

2. Ibid., p. 10.

3. Ibid., pp. 10, 11.

4. Jackson, "Philosophy of PUSH," November 19, 1976.

5. Martin Luther King, Jr., *Where Do We Go from Here: Chaos or Community?* (Boston: Beacon Press, 1967), p. 171.

6. "Program" of PUSH, November 19, 1976.

7. Jackson, "The Present Challenge of Our Democracy: In the Face of Disappointment We Must Act Not Just React." Address to Americans for Democratic Action, 1978, p. 1.

8. Ibid., pp. 2, 3.

9. Jackson, "Challenge of Black Education—Run Faster." Address to the National Alliance of Black School Educators, November 21, 1977, pp. 1-30.

Chapter XIII

1. James H. Cone, *Black Theology and Black Power* (New York: The Seabury Press, 1969), pp. 1, 2.

2. Ibid., p. 151.

3. Cone, *A Black Theology of Liberation* (New York: J. B. Lippincott Co., 1970), p. 17.

4. Ibid., p. 77.

5. Ibid., p. 201.

6. Cone, *God of the Oppressed* (New York: The Seabury Press, 1975), p. 15.

7. *Theology of Liberation*, p. 120.

8. Ibid., p. 124.

9. Ewert H. Cousins, ed., *Hope and the Future of Man* (Philadelphia: Fortress Press, 1972), pp. 56, 57.

10. Ibid., p. 59.

Chapter XIV

1. J. Deotis Roberts, Sr., "A Critique of James H. Cone's *God of the Oppressed*" in *The Journal of the Interdenominational Theological Center* (Fall 1975), p. 58.

2. Roberts, *Liberation and Reconciliation: A Black Theology* (Philadelphia: The Westminster Press, 1971), p. 26.

3. Ibid., pp. 29, 32.

4. Ibid., p. 72.

5. Ibid., p. 79.

6. Ibid., p. 80.

7. Ibid., p. 139.

8. Ibid., p. 140.

Conclusion

1. Charles Shelby Rooks, "Theological Education and the Black Church," *The Christian Century* (February 12, 1969), p. 213.